THE ARCTIC
A GUIDE TO COASTAL WILDLIFE

TONY SOPER
ILLUSTRATIONS BY
DAN POWELL

Bradt Travel Guides, UK
The Globe Pequot Press Inc, USA

Third edition January 2012
First published 2001

Bradt Travel Guides Ltd
IDC House, The Vale, Chalfont St Peter, Bucks SL9 9RZ, England
www.bradtguides.com
Published in the USA by The Globe Pequot Press Inc,
PO Box 480, Guilford, Connecticut 06437-0480

Text copyright © 2012 Tony Soper
Illustrations copyright © 2012 Dan Powell
Maps copyright © 2012 Bradt Travel Guides Ltd
Project manager: Maisie Fitzpatrick

The author and publisher have made every effort to ensure the
accuracy of the information in this book at the time of going to press.
However, they cannot accept any responsibility for any loss,
injury or inconvenience resulting from the use of information
contained in this guide.

British Library Cataloguing in Publication Data
A catalogue record for this book is available from the British Library

ISBN-13: 978 1 84162 380 1

Illustrations Dan Powell
Front cover Pomarine skuas chasing an ivory gull, with polar bear looking on
(Dan Powell)
Photographs Tim Soper 153b, 154; Tony Soper 153a, 154a, 155a, 155b
Maps David McCutcheon

Designed and formatted by Pepenbury Ltd
Production managed by Jellyfish Print Solutions; printed in India

CONTENTS

THE ARCTIC OCEAN

Southern Limit of Continuous Permafrost

Siberia

Summer 10°C Isotherm

Arctic Circle

60°N

Tree Line

New Siberian Islands

Laptev Sea

OCEAN

RUSSIA

Severnaya Zemlya

90°E

Franz Josef Land

Novaya Zemlya

tsbergen

Svalbard

Southern Limit of Pack Ice

Summer 10°C Isotherm

Tree Line

Barents Sea

NORWAY

Murmansk

FINLAND

SWEDEN

AURORA BOREALIS (NORTHERN LIGHTS)

'So tremble the northern lights their silver veil across the heaven, soon gold, soon green, soon reddish; spreading; gathering again in a breathless rush; vibrant illuminated silver threads in exuberant folds; sparkling luminous waves that journey on, and the brilliance lost only for a moment.'

Fridtjof Nansen

Best seen in the winter months when the sun is well below the horizon from a latitude between 60 and 70 degrees, the Aurora takes the form of arcs and beams of pulsating and flickering coloured lights quivering and shimmering and filling the upper sky, in the style of a fluorescent screen. The curtains and draperies of colour may be a mix of yellows, greens, violets and flaming reds, though green auroras are the commonest. Even in high summer there is a fair chance of seeing the effect, though it will be confined to smoky blacks and greys sweeping across the sky.

Auroras (*borealis* and *australis*) are confined to the magnetic pole areas, but they are performances displayed many kilometres high in the sky and stretched over thousands of kilometres wide. They are caused when electrically charged particles streaming towards earth from the sun strike oxygen and hydrogen ions in the rarefied upper atmosphere.

INTRODUCTION

The name 'Arctic' is derived from *arctos*, the Greek for 'bear'. The heavenly constellation of the Great Bear – *Ursa major* – points the way to the Pole Star, *Polaris*. In classical times the region was seen as deliverer of the north wind, *boreas*, bringing the ice and snow of winter to the south, a concept familiar to Mediterranean philosophers long before brave sailors ventured north to prove its existence.

The Arctic is a huge area. There is no clear agreement on its extent, no simple geographical or even political definition of its territory. The 'Arctic Circle' – 66°33'N – may suit cartographers (neatly matching the 'Antarctic Circle' which more naturally defines the Antarctic), but it stretches much too far south, encompassing great industrial cities and vast forests. For oceanographers the Arctic is the region permanently covered by ice, whether it is a vast expanse of solid ice or open water mainly covered by drifting pack; in other words the region where sunlight barely penetrates to the water below and there is little life. Climatologists use isotherms and point to the region north of the 10°C summer isotherm which represents the average temperature in the warmest month of July. This is a concept which also commends itself to biologists, for it positions the Arctic conveniently north of the tree line. It is the definition we have adopted for this book.

The permanent ice of the Arctic is a three- or four-metre thick sheet covering eight million square kilometres north of Svalbard and Franz Josef Land. The rivers of ice coming down from the Greenland ice cap end as glaciers, the most impressive in the northern hemisphere; the largest carve great icebergs into Disko Bay on the west coast, lesser ones go to sea from Scoresby Sound in east Greenland, Svalbard and Franz Josef Land.

Polar bear stargazing

The Arctic is cold, below freezing point for more than half the year, and it is dry – a region of high winds and little rainfall. Parts are as arid as the Sahara: in northwest Greenland the annual precipitation is

7

75mm (London enjoys 550mm). But the seasonal retreat of the ice provides an ice-edge effect. The returning sun encourages algae to form under the ice, to be browsed by crustaceans; increasing warmth fuels plant plankton in the open waters of the polynyas and around the edge of the ice. The ocean is surrounded by a shallow continental shelf whose nutrient-rich surface waters encourage a plankton bloom which nourishes the fish, seabirds, seals and whales which visit to take advantage of the summer harvest, when the peripheral ice retreats in the face of warm water from the south. From diatoms to great whales the coastal waters produce a seasonal abundance. The Arctic flora and fauna are adapted to these violently fluctuating living conditions but the ecological balance is fragile, easily disturbed and slow to recover.

The Arctic landscape is characterised by year-round permafrost, where only the surface thaws for a short period in the summer. There are clearly defined seasons; the cold dark days of winter, when the temperature rarely exceeds freezing, lasts the best part of nine months; summer arrives with a rush, bringing warmth and almost continuous daylight from May to July. This is when the ground-hugging plants bloom and insects flourish to fuel the breeding of an immense immigration of birds. By the middle of August most of them have retreated south, away from the onset of the ice. Spring and autumn are short and sweet.

Defining the Arctic could become an academic pastime – its influence spreads way beyond whatever imaginary line is drawn around it. But for the purposes of this introduction to the wildlife, we have considered the interests of those intrepid explorers who penetrate the icy wilderness by sea, landing only on its coastal edges.

'Give me dogs, give me winter, and you can keep the rest'
Knut Rasmussen

EXPLOITATION AND CONSERVATION

T housands of years ago the hunter-gatherers of the Siberian coast pioneered east across Bering to colonise Alaska and northern Canada, eventually finding themselves in Greenland. Coming the other way, in the 7th and 8th centuries, Irish monks may have been the first Europeans to penetrate north and west. They sailed sturdy ox-hide curraghs and founded communities in the Hebrides, the Faroes and in Iceland, paving the way for a North Atlantic 'stepping stone' passage which may have taken the first Europeans to North America. Certainly the Vikings of Scandinavia were not far behind, exploring and colonising in the 9th and 10th centuries, sustained by plentiful fish and seabirds. They established permanent colonies in Greenland, before penetrating even further west to settle in Newfoundland. In the 14th century the Basque whalers who hunted sperm and right whales in the Bay of Biscay started to explore further into the North Atlantic and established themselves on the coast of

St Brendan with his Irish monks on passage to Iceland in the 7th or 8th century, preparing for Mass on the back of a fin whale. From Plautius, Caspar 'Nova Typis Transacto Navigo': Venice, 1621

9

Labrador. Much later, British and Dutch fishermen were to learn from the Basques, take their techniques north, and the rot set in for what was once a great stock of whales.

Arctic wildlife flourished in abundance until the great 16th-century age of exploration and discovery. Explorers were not, of course, exploring solely for the love of knowledge. The spirit of scientific curiosity led naturally to the pursuit of monetary gain, with merchants anxious to discover more profitable routes to the East. The land route from Western Europe to China was difficult and dangerous, while the sea route via the Cape was long. Therefore the prospect of a northern sea route was attractive enough to encourage speculative exploration. In 1586 John Davis set sail from Dartmouth in *Ellen* for his third attempt on 'the search and discoverie of the north-west passage to China'. Crossing the strait by this time named after him, he reached into Cumberland Sound before having to turn home. But his favourable reports encouraged others to attempt the passage through to the Pacific. This was finally achieved by the Norwegian, Amundsen, in 1905 with *Gjoa*.

It was the Dutch who first explored the other prospective trade route to the Pacific. In 1594, the last decade of the 16th century, the greatest of all Dutch seamen, Willem Barents, sailed in *Mercury* in search of the putative Northeast Passage. By this time the Dutch already had a thriving commerce in furs and timber with the Russian port of Archangel. Barents reached Novaya Zemlya in the sea which is now named after him, but turned back in the face of impenetrable ice. On his third attempt, sailing from Amsterdam, he discovered Bear Island and Svalbard, reaching Spitsbergen on 17 June 1596. Gerrit de Veer, an officer who had sailed with him on all three voyages, kept a diary in which he recorded encounters with the 'great white beare'.

Willem Barents

'The 21 of June we cast out our anchor at 18 fathoms before the land; and then we and John Cornelysons men rowed on the west side of the land, and there fetched ballast. When we got on board again we saw a white beare that swam towards our shippe, whereupon we left off our worke, and entering into the boat rowed after her, and crossing her in the way, drove her from the land, wherewith she swamme further into the sea... she swam a mile into the sea, yet we followed her with the most part of all our men of both shippes in three boats,

Theodore de Bry

and struck oftentimes at her, cutting and hewing her, so that all our armes were most broken in peeces. During our fight with her, she struck her claws so hard in our boate that the signs thereof were seen in it, but as hap was, it was in the forehead of our boate, for if it had been in the middle thereof, she had peradventure overthrown it, they have such force in their claws. At last we overcame her, her skinne being 13 foote long.'

In 1607 the British navigator Henry Hudson sailed north in Hopewell, again aiming to find a sea route east towards China and Japan but hoping that it was possible to sail across the top of the world. He explored Svalbard and discovered Jan Mayen, at the same time finding a wealth of whales. Inevitably trade, in the form of whalers and sealers, followed the flag. Bowheads were the main prey, but bears, seals and walruses, to say nothing of countless numbers of seabirds, were all grist to the mill. Whale oil was greatly in demand in Western Europe. Known as 'train-oil', it was used in making candles, for lamps, lubricants and soap, and, at a later stage, for street lighting.

At first the whalers caught and processed their catch at sea, learning from the Basques. But by 1613 a number of vessels were exploring whaling possibilities on the shores of Spitsbergen. Hostilities between English and Dutch ended with an agreement whereby the British whalers from Hull worked the more convenient southerly waters and the Dutch took the northwest.

The whaling station at Smeerenburg. Cornelis de Man, 1639

The Dutch were first to set up a shore station, on Amsterdam Island. Smeerenburg – Blubber City – was established round about 1620. At first the whalers lived in campsite conditions, but as time went by paved streets served a dozen or so sturdy houses. There were eight double ovens in the tryworks. The settlement was protected from the marauding Brits by the cannons of a small fort.

After the disastrous experiences of a few pioneering winterers, the station was operated only by a summer population of about 200. Most of their food came with them from the Netherlands, but it was of poor quality, made palatable with a liberal spread of mustard. To remain healthy the whalers took advantage of local fish and birds, eggs and the occasional reindeer. Nearby colonies of little auks deposited quantities of nitrogen-rich excrement on the scree slopes, nourishing the scurvy-grass which protected them from disease. Ice conditions changed for the worse in the mid-17th century and the whalers were forced to abandon the shore station, flensing the whales alongside their ships and taking the blubber back to Europe for cooking.

Even so, the enterprise was hugely profitable. Between 1675 and 1721 the Dutch employed a total of 5,886 ships and took 32,907 whales, at an average value of £900 each – an enormous profit. By the early

'In one of my earliest voyages to the whale-fishery, I observed a circumstance which excited my highest astonishment. One of our harpooners had struck a whale, it dived, and all the assisting boats had collected round the fast-boat, before it arose to the surface. The first boat which approached it advanced incautiously upon it. It rose with unexpected violence beneath the boat, and projected it and all its crew, to the height of some yards in the air. It fell on its side, upset, and cast all the men into the water. One man received a severe blow... the rest of the boat's crew escaped without any hurt'.

William Scoresby, *An Account of the Arctic Regions*, Constable, 1820

William Scoresby was witness to the incident recorded in this engraving.

Oh, the lookout on the mainmast stood
With a spyglass in his hand.
'There's a whale, there's a whale, and a whale-fish,' he cried,
'And she blows at every span, brave boys,
And she blows at every span.'

Now the harpoon struck and the lines played out,
But she gave such a flourish with her tail,
She capsized our boat and we lost five men,
And we could not catch that whale, brave boys,
And we could not catch that whale.

'The Greenland Whale Fishery',
folksong first recorded in 1725

years of the 18th century there were more than 200 whaling vessels, mostly Dutch, but also British, German and Danish, chasing the bowheads.

The pressure of hunting was devastating and the bowheads were unable to take the strain; in two hundred years they were brought near to extinction. By the middle of the 18th century the whaling station at Smeerenburg was abandoned (today only the remains of the ovens are to be seen). The whalers turned their attentions to the whale stocks of the Davis Strait and Baffin Bay off West Greenland, a fishery which flourished well into the 19th century.

Polar wildlife suffered greatly from the impact of human discovery. The great Arctic abundance of seals and whales was exploited mercilessly from the early 17th century. Bowheads were the first to succumb, but other whale populations were drastically reduced by the early part of the 20th century. Walrus and other seals were hunted from the early days of exploration, though as with polar bears most intensively from the early 19th. Protection measures in the mid-20th century, in response to the increased effectiveness of whaling provided by Sven Foyne's devastating harpoon gun, came in time to reverse the trend in most cases. But recovery of the Arctic whales, if it comes at all, will take many years, and, only too predictably, whalers are currently concentrating on the alleged abundance of minkes.

Polar bears face an uncertain future in a melting world, though at least they are protected by law from safari hunters. Walruses, though on their knees, are recovering. The eider ducks which were taken for their down, their eggs and their chicks and as adults, are thriving. The Svalbard reindeer, which from a population of many thousands were reduced to a couple of hundred by the 1920s, are flourishing under Norwegian protection. Arctic animals are, however, recovering only slowly from centuries of ill-considered harvesting.

Walrus hunting. From Sir William Jardine, 'The Naturalist's Library', vol VI, London, 1839

The hope is that intelligent monitoring of wildlife resources may lead to a programme of sustainable harvesting in the Arctic. But of course there are always new threats. Wildlife tourism is a potential hazard in ecologically vulnerable areas and requires sensitive management. On the one hand tourists may cause disturbance, yet on the other wilderness tourism can be a positive force for education towards a better understanding of the need for protection and wise use of resources. Subsistence whaling by native communities can be a force for intelligent management in Nunavut, Greenland and Siberia. The alternative of fast boats and powerful rifles makes for improved catch rates and an even greater requirement for agreed quotas.

Legal protection of the Arctic flora and fauna is aimed at ensuring the conservation of biological diversity and sustainable use. The Ramsar Convention (on wetlands of international importance especially as waterfowl habitat) has as its object the reduction of loss of wetlands, encouragement of understanding of the ecological function of wetlands and their economic, cultural, scientific and recreational value. At the other end of the scale, the International Whaling Commission (IWC) aims to regulate the harvesting of marine mammals. Commercial whaling has an unhappy record of poor resource management and naked greed, and the challenge that has always faced the IWC is to monitor stocks and set quotas which are realistic enough to ensure a healthy future for whales.

Powerful icebreakers make it possible for adventurous tourists to explore the High Arctic, and increase environmental awareness

PLANTS

The first surprise in landing on an Arctic beach is the paucity of littoral plants. The beach is bare of seaweeds; in fact, it is remarkably bare, except for a profusion of current-borne Siberian timber. Where you expect to see various wracks and low-water kelps, there is nothing but a beach scraped clean by moving ice. To find evidence of marine plants it would be necessary to dive down a few feet in the cold water to depths below the influence of the surface ice which scours the tideline. Once you get behind the beach, though, there is a profusion of special plants. In Svalbard, for instance, there are over 150 species of highly adapted plants. On the northern side of the coniferous taiga lies the tundra – barren and almost treeless. In fact the Arctic willow *Salix polaris* and dwarf birch *Betula nana* survive here only by virtue of being small and stunted, ground-hugging and barely ankle-high. Polar scurvy grass *Cochlearia groenlandica* flourishes and grows tallest when fertilised under seabird colonies, whose droppings are rich in organic nitrogen and phosphates.

Arctic willow
(actual size)
A root 2cm in
diameter may
be several
centuries old.

The landscape of the high Arctic is determined by the permafrost – where it is continuous the ground is frozen down for several hundred metres. Only in the summer is the top metre melted enough to create a poorly drained marshy soil with a certain amount of dry country. Arctic plants must therefore adapt to the harsh conditions of winter, when there is intense frost, yet endure summer temperatures which may reach as high as 30°C. Mosses and lichens abound.

SVALBARD

Purple saxifrage,
Saxifraga oppositifolia,
a low mat-forming
perennial with
trailing stems. Grows
on damp and stony
scree. First to bloom
in the Arctic spring.

Arctic saxifrage,
S. nivalis, identified by
its white or pink spotless
flowers. It grows in
shaded rock ledges in
scree or moraine.

Arctic cotton grass,
Eriophorum scheuchzeri,
a tussock-forming
sedge which grows
in wet bogs.

Snow buttercup,
Ranunculus nivalis,
a tiny perennial which
grows on the tundra
and rocky ledges.

GREENLAND

Most of the coastal plants in Greenland are from a vegetational community called 'dwarf shrub heath'.

Crowberry, *Empetrum nigrum*, an evergreen dwarf shrub which dominates the outer coastal heaths. Early flowering, with tasty fruits.

Arctic blueberry, *Vaccinium uliginosum*, the most common dwarf shrub along with willow and birch. It is able to grow on windswept ridges, clinging on even when the snow blanket is blown off.

Narrow-leaved Labrador tea, *Ledum palustre*, a common fragrant dwarf shrub found on mossy heaths and bogs. It has deliciously aromatic leaves – you really can make tea out of them.

NB Bering Sea plants are on page 142

Blue or mountain heath, *Phyllodoce coerulea*, grows in heaths with medium snow cover, especially in coastal areas.

INVERTEBRATES

Polar waters are rich in invertebrates, except under permanent ice. While there may be a short-lived bloom of diatoms under the ice, the three summer months of great abundance occur only in the more ice-free waters. And it is there that the vast quantities of zooplankton fuel the summer influx of birds and whales.

Drift-ice and floes are home for the kind of plant life which supports invertebrates. A brown 'scum', *Mellosira arctica*, grows on the underside of the ice, producing floating strands which may be several metres long. This ice algae provides food for the herbivorous plankton which in turn provides food for the tiny carnivores; all of them are eaten by the fish, birds, seals and whales. It is true that there is low species-diversity in polar waters, but nevertheless there is enough year-round food for a few exceptionally well-adapted birds and even a few mammals to survive on a year-round basis.

Whereas tropical waters are relatively barren, open polar waters in summer attract a vast temporary population of seabirds, which feed on the copepods, shrimps and fish larvae, and whales, which cruise in leisurely pursuit of armadas of sea snails. This is especially true of the interface where warm Atlantic water reaches into high northern latitudes by way of the North Atlantic Drift.

Butterfly snail,
Clione limacina
(lifesize)

In late summer vast swarms of sea snails travel on the North Atlantic Drift and find themselves in high latitudes, where they graze on the phytoplankton. These pteropods often occur in such large swarms that they discolour the surface. They

Winged snail,
Limacina helicina
(lifesize)

represent a vital food source for the great bowhead whales, which engulf and sieve them through their baleen plates. On a calm day in coastal waters, they may be found just under the surface, flying along with their two fins, lobe-like modifications of their feet.

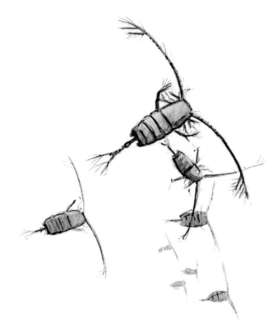

Uncountable numbers of tiny copepods flourish in the plankton.

Scoop a handful of sea and you will find several of them in your hand, protected by a thin, delicate shell in the case of the winged snail. The butterfly snail is a shell-less 'naked pteropod' which may grow to as much as 36mm in length in the far north.

For sheer abundance, copepods rule the world; they are the most important link in the marine food chain, eaten by almost everything from fish to birds to whales. With antennae at the bow and a tail at the stern, they progress in a stately fashion by paddling with their legs (copepod means 'oar-footed', from the Greek *kope* – oar). Several millimetres long, the northern species *Calanus finmarchicus* represents a major food source for little auks. While they may be small, more-or-less transparent, with only a few spots of bright scarlet for decoration, they exist in astronomical and nourishing numbers, good news for little auks and great whales.

In polar regions copepods may reach a centimetre in length.

FISH

As sunlight increases in intensity towards the summer months, Arctic phytoplankton thrives and increases mightily, to be grazed by the zooplankton whose shrimps and water-hoppers are taken by the Arctic cod. Under the ice-floes the algae blossoms and in turn is harvested by the free-floating plankton. The sea becomes a rich soup supporting vast numbers of fishes – salmon, char, capelin as well as the cod find a living in cold Arctic waters – although there are relatively few fish species which can survive in these latitudes. As with the birds, there may be a paucity of species, but they are here in large numbers. Specially adapted to these cold waters, polar fish have anti-freeze in their blood systems which prevents them from freezing solid.

1m

Greenland shark, *Somniosus microcephalus*
Largest of the dogfishes, this is the most northerly shark. Often seen at the surface, it may be as much as 6.5m in length overall. Much prized by the Inuit, the liver was used for fuel oil and the dried flesh for dog food (the fresh flesh is poisonous, and quite apart from that disadvantage it reeks of ammonia, since the shark urinates through its flesh). It has an 'interesting' taste, much appreciated in Iceland after fermentation as Hákarl.

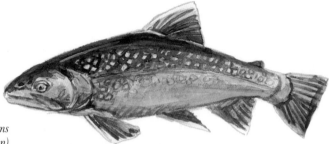

Length to 40cms
(16in)

Arctic char, *Salvelinus alpinus*
The most truly arctic of all fish, and also the most prized by
the ship's galley. As with salmon, they spend most of the
year at sea, entering fresh water only to spawn, when they
are spectacularly colourful, pale pink to bright red. They
reach to 81°N in Lake Hazen on Ellesmere Island in the
Canadian Arctic.

Length to 25cms
(10in)

Polar cod, *Boreogadus saida*
A circumpolar species, living its entire life in near-zero
temperatures. The juvenile fry feed on copepods and the algae
growing under ice-floes, while the adults take amphipods,
shrimps and other crustaceans. It is taken by narwhals,
belugas, ringed seals and seabirds. Small in size, it must be
the only codfish not subject to commercial fishery, though
some are taken by the Russians.

Length to 20cms
(8in)

Capelin, *Mallotus villosus*
A key species, preyed upon by cod, seabirds, seals and whales.
Subject to large-scale fluctuations in population, sometimes
due to overfishing, sometimes to natural consequences of
changes in sea temperature and currents.

BIRDS

The Arctic is seasonally home to some of the largest seabird populations in the world. It has been estimated that some 16 million individuals summer in the Barents Sea. One hundred and eighty three species of birds breed in high latitudes, taking advantage of the short but immensely productive summer season of insect abundance. As the sunlight returns in spring, the burgeoning life at the edge of the ice, under the floes and in the open waters of the polynyas, supports a huge influx of birds from the south.

Polynyas are areas of water which are open throughout the year, sometimes large and long-lasting, sometimes small and temporary. They are immensely important as feeding places for birds, seals and whales.

The immigrants are well adapted to the harsh realities of Arctic life. Feathers are well designed not only for flight but as good insulators. The plumage of the very few resident Arctic birds is denser than that of seasonal visitors. In extreme cold, birds will tuck both their legs and heads under the feathers. Snow buntings and ptarmigans dig snowholes in order to crouch out of the wind. Courtship tends to be brief, with nests constructed and eggs laid at the earliest possible moment, since the summer season of plenty is short. A late thaw may even mean that whole populations of seabirds fail to breed successfully. Eiders and terns must wait until the ice breaks up to expose the ground and isolate their offshore islands from the predatory foxes. Incoming geese, ducks and waders (shorebirds) may court, nest and lay within days of arrival. They take maximum advantage of the 24 hours of daylight. Ross's gulls, ivory gulls and Brünnich's guillemots show specific adaptations to the environment and depend on ice fauna for much of their food. The auks in general tend to time their arrival at the breeding cliffs as the winter ice breaks up and the increased day length encourages phytoplankton growth in the sea. At hatching time in midsummer the inshore waters offer plentiful zooplankton, such as copepods, for the growing chicks.

Ptarmigan feet are well-feathered to keep them warm; they also act as snowshoes.

Some 50 species of waders breed in the Arctic, some reaching very high latitudes – Baird's sandpiper may nest as high as 80° north from the Canadian Arctic to Siberia. Sanderlings, purple sandpipers and turnstones are similarly circumpolar. (But for the purposes of this book we have concentrated only on the two waders most easily seen along the coast.)

Summer breeders tend to be off on their migrations to the milder south by the end of August, though fulmar fledglings are likely to be still on their ledges till early September.

Seabird populations are notoriously subject to violent fluctuations. In the Arctic a late break-up of the ice may deny food to breeding birds and cause mass starvation. At the other end of the season, if the few days of autumn arrive early, juveniles may be unable to fly from the onset of winter. The autumn moult may even be delayed in order to make an early getaway and leave winter behind. Geese returning to their winter quarters in the south may arrive without the expected proportion of young goslings, evidence of a poor breeding season. Snowy owls will not breed at all in a year when lemmings are scarce.

Survival of human populations, such as the Inuit, depended, and still to a certain extent, depends, on the summer influx of birds. They are an important food source, but also provide materials for clothing and bedding.

Glaucous gulls are major predators in the Arctic.

RED-THROATED DIVER
(Red-throated loon, rain goose)
Gavia stellata

Red-throated divers are the smallest, the most northerly and the most widespread of the divers. Circumpolar, breeding on the Arctic and subarctic tundra to 83° north, mainly along the coastal fringe of the Canadian Arctic, Greenland, Svalbard and east to Siberia. They have characteristic long necks in flight, with uptilted beaks while on the water. They prey on small fish, pursued underwater – in Arctic waters taking mostly polar cod, butterfish and capelin.

They arrive at the breeding areas in May, but stay at sea till the ice breaks up on the freshwater lakes and ponds where they nest. They come ashore only for breeding, sometimes solo, sometimes in small colonies. In June they go to freshwater pools, sometimes large lakes, with a profusion of bankside vegetation. The nest is a flattened patch of greenery or sometimes a mossy, weedy heap, very close to the water so that the birds can slide in and out with ease. Their legs are set well back on the body and they are

*Length
53–69cm
(22–29in)*

*Wingspan
106–116cm
(44–48in)*

somewhat clumsy on land. The clutch is usually of two eggs, incubated by both parents for 24 to 29 days. At this stage they are vulnerable to disturbance. If all goes well the newly hatched chicks leave the nest on their second day, already able to swim, cared for by both parents. They fledge at 43 days, when they are independent and go to sea.

Red-throated divers winter south to the coast of America and the coast of Norway and at points south to the Iberian peninsula. In the British Isles they have been known from the ice age fossil record but more recently as winter visitors, now widespread, since the 18th century.

The red-throat is the most northerly loon. As a breeding bird the larger white-throated diver G. adamsii is confined to the coast below 78°N.

They were historically known as loons in the Shetland Isles and southern Ireland (Ray 1678, 'the greater loon or arsefoot'). Literally meaning 'fool', loon is a corruption of the Norse *lómr*; the wailing call of the bird spawned the Icelandic *lómur* – 'moan' – 'a most mournful and eerie, long-drawn, mewing wail or shriek, like the cry of a person in extreme pain'. Present-day Scandinavian usage is *lom* – pronounced 'loom'. Loon is now the accepted and much-appreciated North American name for 'diver'.

TRADITIONAL CLOTHING

Bird skins have traditionally been used by Arctic peoples for articles of clothing, luggage, rugs and children's toys, among other things! Feather-covered skin coats have been found on the mummified bodies of Inuit women. In one case the skins of white-fronted goose, cormorant, eider and mallard were used for the body part of a coat, while the hood was made from red-throated diver skins.

NORTHERN FULMAR
(Mollymawk)
Fulmarus glacialis

The name 'fulmar' comes from the Norse, meaning 'foul gull', from its musty smell and habit of spitting noisome stomach oil at aggressors. Fulmars, belonging to the petrel family, are superficially gull-like but stockier and bull-necked, with a stubby tubenose bill and, at close range, a dark eye. In flight they behave like a small albatross interspersing flapping with much stiff-winged gliding, the leading edge of the wing being straight as opposed to the bow-shape of gulls. They have grey upperparts with pale-blue wrist-patches.

The fulmar is a prime example of a polymorphic species, in which two distinct forms exist in one interbreeding population (see also *skuas*). The variation is genetically based and not a distinction based on sex. In the case of the fulmar, the proportion of the darker so-called 'blue phase' individuals increases with latitude further north. As is the case with the skuas, these polymorphic species are characteristic of

Length
45–50cm
(19–21in)

Wingspan
102–112cm
(43–47in)

the Arctic, for reasons which remain unexplained – there is no evidence that there is any advantage one way or another in terms of breeding success; birds representing one morph will happily mate with the other. The phenomenon was first recorded by the Dutchman Friedrich Martens, who sailed north in 1671 with the Hamburg vessel *Jonas im Walfisch*. He described the 'blue' form as the commonest birds in Spitsbergen, noting that they were unlike the grey fulmars he knew from Scotland and Norway. Fulmars were seen as far north as 85°05' north in 1895 by Fridtjof Nansen, when he was well north of Franz Josef Land on his attempt to reach the North Pole by sledge, having left *Fram* deliberately beset in the ice, drifting from the New Siberian Islands to Spitsbergen over two winters. In fact, fulmars will follow an icebreaker all the way to the North Pole, taking advantage of the plankton disturbed by the screws.

'This that you see here I did design among the ice.'
Friedrich Martens,
1 June 1671

Fulmars are confirmed ship-followers, sometimes in large flocks. In the Arctic whaling days, they gathered at the carcasses tearing blubber till they could swallow no more. More recently they followed trawlers to gorge on the offal and by-catch thrown over the side. Fuelled by this sort of food availability, they colonised ever further south, breeding freely as far south as southern Britain but north as far as 80°, taking advantage of the polynya at the northeasternmost corner of Greenland.

Fulmars have been greatly exploited through the years by island communities as a useful food resource. Thomas Pennant wrote of the community of St Kilda in 1776: 'No bird is of such use to the islanders as this: the Fulmar supplies them with oil for their lamps, down for their beds, a delicacy for their tables, a balm for their wounds and a medicine for their distempers.'

In courtship fulmars indulge in water-dances, noisy displays by as many as a dozen birds on the water close to the nesting cliffs. At the nest site itself – a mere scrape on a convenient ledge – they can also be noisy. They breed colonially on the greener parts of coastal cliffs and inland nunataks, provided there is easy access to open seas. Like all petrels, they lay a single white egg, incubated for 50 days, the young fledging in six to eight weeks. The adults range far over the Barents Sea as well as both the North Atlantic and Pacific, but have a strong attachment to their nest-place, often visiting it outside the breeding season. Young birds disperse to live at sea for several years before returning to their birthplace to prospect for a nest site.

Island people harvested fulmars as an important survival resource, not only for eggs and meat. The feathers provided bedding (said to be impervious to lice and bedbugs), the entrails were used for bait in fishing, the bones consigned to the midden to become fertiliser, and the stomach used for oil (half a pint from every carcass) for medicine and winter lighting.

'The fulmar is the constant companion of the whale-fisher. It joins his ship immediately on passing the Shetland Islands, and accompanies it through the trackless ocean to the highest accessible latitudes. It keeps an eager watch for any thing thrown overboard; the smallest particle of fatty substance can scarcely escape it. As such, a hook baited with a piece of fat meat or blubber, and towed by a long twine over the ship's stern, is a means employed by the sailor-boys for taking them.'

William Scoresby,
An account of the Arctic Regions, Constable, 1820.

Engraving by Thomas Bewick 1847

OIL SECRETION AND EXCRETION
In addition to the large tail glands which yield oil for preening, all members of the petrel family, from the mighty albatross to the sparrow-sized storm petrel, regurgitate stomach oil through the mouth and nostrils. In the fulmars, the evil-smelling fluid may shoot several feet towards an intruder. It has an unpleasantly strong musky odour which clings persistently to the petrel and its nesting place (and to human flesh and clothes). The main function of this vomiting is to lighten the bird for easier escape. The skunk-like habit of squirting a stinking fluid may have developed as a supplementary defence as the fulmars nest in open, vulnerable situations.

The oil appears only in the stomachs of nesting petrels, disappearing when the chicks are bigger and are being fed more solid semi-digested marine organisms; it is in effect a store of baby-food of the right consistency. Despite its powerful smell, it is perfectly digestible, and used in preparation of food by Polynesian and other peoples.

NORTHERN GANNET
Morus bassanas

Length
86–96cm
(34–38in)

Wingspan
165–180cm
(65–72in)

The largest and most spectacular of North Atlantic seabirds, gannets forage far north of their breeding colonies in Iceland and Norway, reaching to Jan Mayen and even towards Franz Josef Land in the summer.

Gannets appear 'whiter than white' at a distance and 'pointed at both ends' when close, with conspicuous black wing-tips. Their bodies are cigar-shaped and they have long, fairly narrow wings, wedge-shaped tails, stout bills and forward-facing eyes. Gannets are plunge-divers, are powerful in flight, and are double-breasted, with air sacs between the skins to absorb impact when they dive from 10m or more in pursuit of fast pelagic fish like herrings. First marking their chosen prey from the air, they close their wings to drop vertically into the water. Specially adapted for this activity, with forward vision and slit nostrils, gannets strike the surface with great force, sending up a tremendous splash and continuing their dive underwater using their feet and wings. The catch may be swallowed underwater or it may be brought to the surface. Usually the dive is brief and the buoyant bird rises, takes off, then circles to dive again.

BRENT GOOSE

(Brant)

Branta bernicla

A high Arctic 'black goose', with a voice like a growling croak, the Brent has a sooty black head, chest and upper back. The rest is dark grey-brown except for the white upper tail coverts and a small white patch either side of the neck. The bill, legs and feet are black. Its range overlaps with that of the barnacle, and there is much confusion between the two, but the barnacle has a much whiter face. They float high in the water with a cocked-up tail and are fast, manoeuvrable fliers with a short rapid beat of narrow wings. They may easily be confused with large ducks but have shorter necks and narrower wings, showing a white V in the tail as they fly low and close-packed over the water in an ungooselike fashion.

There are two races: dark-bellied Brents breed both in Arctic Russia/Siberia and Alaska/Canada; while the light-bellied race breeds in Greenland/Svalbard/Franz Josef Land.

*Length
56–66cm
(23–28in)*

*Wingspan
110–120cm
(46–50in)*

They breed colonially on low-lying tundra close to the sea. In Svalbard, where they were once common, they are now rare and confined to the Tusenøyane (Thousand Islands) south of Edgeøya in the southeast. In Greenland and Arctic Canada they tend to nest close to a snowy owl in the hope of protection from predators. If the owls suffer a poor lemming year, when they fail to breed, the Arctic foxes move in on the geese. Their nests are normally close to water – a shallow depression lined with grass and moss and with a generous inner lining of down which covers the eggs when the goose takes time off. They lay three to five eggs, with incubation about 25 days, and fledging in 40 days. Sexual maturity, as with barnacles, takes two to three years.

The dark-bellied Brents winter on estuaries in eastern Britain, the Netherlands and the Atlantic coast of France – the light race in eastern North America, Ireland and around Denmark. They tend to roost at sea, seldom far inland, giving rise to the name sea-goose.

In their wintering grounds Brent geese feed extensively on eel-grass, *Zostera marina*, and, in spring, glasswort, *Salicornia*. They suffered a catastrophic decline in the 1930s, when their winter feed of eel-grass was hit by disease. Being something of a boom-or-bust species, they have recovered dramatically and in the process have altered their behaviour to the extent that they are now regarded as an agricultural problem, coming inland during the tidal high-water period in tight, fast-moving flocks to sample winter wheat at its most active growth period, when there is the maximum protein and nitrogen in the growing tips. They are particularly clever at selecting grass fields which have been treated with high levels of nitrogen fertiliser. With their short bills they are able to take advantage of the sward before it is long enough for cattle and sheep. A single goose may eat roughly half a pound (dry weight) of grass a day.

'The Arctic trails have their secret tales
That would make your blood run cold'
Robert Service

BARNACLE GOOSE
Branta leucopsis

A white-faced 'black goose' which yelps like a dog, the barnacle goose is the most coastal of all geese. A truly Arctic bird, breeding nowhere else in the world; there are three distinct populations: in east Greenland, Svalbard and Novaya Zemlya.

Low-lying islands, craggy islets and sea-cliff ledges are the preferred nest places, the criterion being protection from the marauding Arctic foxes. Probably in earlier times they nested on the tundra, but fox predation has encouraged them to retreat to the coast. They arrive at the colony in May, laying their clutch of four or five eggs as soon as there is open water nearby. Incubation takes 24–5 days – the gander stands guard while the goose sits. Once hatched, the family moves

Length
58–71cm
(24–30in)

Wingspan
132–145cm
(55–60in)

to areas of abundant vegetation, grazing dwarf willow, *Salix polaris,* on the coastal meadows, often in large flocks. Fledging occurs in 40–45 days. In July or August the geese moult, always close to water to which they run in their flightless condition if disturbed. Once their fat reserves are replenished after the moult, they migrate south to avoid the harsh Arctic winter. In flight, flocks adopt a more sickle-shaped formation than the conventional V-shape of most waterfowl.

The Greenland population winters on the Outer Hebrides (mainly on Islay) and the northwest coast of Ireland, the Svalbard birds winter in the Solway Firth of Scotland. The Siberian birds winter along the coast of the Netherlands, encouraged by enlightened protection. All the separate populations declined in the early 20th century but more recently have been recovering. The world population is around 100,000, of which a third winter in the British Isles.

How did it get its name? Which came first, goose or barnacle? Was it bird or fish? See opposite...

FISH OR FOWL?

The barnacle goose has a curious claim to fame. In early times, no one knew where the birds bred; their arrival every autumn was regarded as something of a mystery, explained only by a bizarre link with a marine crustacean – the goose barnacle *Lepas anatifera*. Commonly thrown ashore attached to floating branches or driftwood, goose barnacles do bear a striking resemblance to the neck and beak of a bird, complete with 'feathers' in the shape of their filter mechanisms, the *cirri*.

The popular myth held that no egg or nest was involved in the development of the bird but that the infant stage of the barnacle geese was generated spontaneously and nourished by trees. At a time when dietary laws were more closely followed by the religious, the advantage of believing in the maritime origin of the fat bird was obvious. Coming from the sea, the barnacle goose could safely be classified as fish, suitable for the table on a Friday.

'Bishops and religious men in some parts of Ireland do not scruple to dine off these birds at a time of fasting because they are not flesh nor born of flesh.'

Giraldus Cambrensis, 1185

The tradition flourished till Pope Innocent III forbade the practice by decree in the 12th century, but it lingered for several centuries more in the remoter parts of Ireland.

'The story of the myth still fascinates for the light it sheds on the credulity and mendacity of scholars.'
Edward Armstrong, 1958

'Certain trees bear fruit which, decaying within, produces a worm which, as it subsequently developes, becomes hairy and feathered, and, provided wings, flies like a bird.'

John Gerard,
Herball, or Generall Historie of Plantes, 1597

LONG-TAILED DUCK
(Old squaw)
Clangula hyemalis

*Length
40–47cm
(17–20in)*

*Wingspan
73–79cm
(30–33in)*

Circumpolar in the high Arctic, the long-tailed duck is a common and widespread species, though there are relatively few in Svalbard, where solitary pairs breed on small islands, often alongside Arctic terneries. Long tails are, not surprisingly, the chief characteristic of the drake. Plumage is black, chestnut and white in summer. *Clangula* in the scientific name comes from the Latin *clangor* for noisy – which is certainly true of this duck. The once-ubiquitous American name 'old squaw', an indelicate reference to its garrulous gossiping, is now politically incorrect. At the breeding grounds they indulge in wild aerial displays when the drakes belt out a lusty *ack-ar-de-lak*. *Hyemalis* is latin for winter, which is when most of us see them.

They congregate around small tundra pools, boggy places and rivers, sometimes beside the sea, especially in rocky fjords. Loosely colonial at the breeding sites, they choose a natural depression among vegetation on open ground. Six to nine eggs are laid as soon as the site is ice-free in May or June, and incubation is by the female for 24–9 days, during which the male plays no part. Ducklings leave the nest soon after hatching, to be taken to a freshwater pond and subsequently to sea. Fledging takes 35–40 days.

Food is whatever is on offer in the local pool. But on the coast they take molluscs and crustaceans, sea urchins, small fish and some vegetation. They are expert divers, reaching depths of at least 30m, though normal dives are less than 10m on an average dive of 30–60 seconds.

In winter long-tailed ducks are wholly maritime, mostly offshore in large rafts, as far south as the Baltic and the British Isles in Europe and South Carolina in North America. While perhaps two million individuals winter in the western palearctic, the total world population of long-tailed duck may exceed ten million. At present they seem not to be threatened in conservation terms. However, since they have a roosting tendency to gather in large rafts at sea, they may be vulnerable to oil spills. Many drown in fishing nets, many are hunted by shooters on their migrations in Canada and North America. A freshly killed long-tailed duck is said to contain 1mg of vitamin C in every 100mg eaten!

COMMON EIDER
(Cuddy duck)

Somateria mollissima

Length
50–71cm
(21–30in)

Wingspan
80–108cm
(33–45in)

Common eiders are heavily built diving ducks, with handsome black-and-white colouring. In profile, both sexes have strikingly wedge-shaped beaks and heads – distinctly sloping with the tip of the beak sloping up to the top of the head without a curve.

A marine species, these are coastal sea-ducks which breed on islands along low-lying rocky coasts, wherever ice permits access to the shore. They arrive at the breeding grounds in early spring, but wait till the islands are free of ice to begin nesting activity. Generally colonial, they make a saucer shape on the ground, starting a nest with vegetable material and lining it generously with down feathers pulled from the duck's own breast and flanks. The nest is often in the lee of a feature such as a rock or tideline debris. Usually four to six eggs are laid in May or even later in the year further north. As with the Brent geese, the eiders often associate their colonies with a snowy owl nest, to gain protection from predatory foxes. There is an element of mutual benefit: the geese warn the owl of the appproach of the fox, the owl won't allow a fox anywhere near its nest.

Eider eggs have been taken in large numbers by Greenlanders and others, as for instance the Scots and English whalers in earlier times. In Greenland the Inuit of the Upernavik district took eggs freely till they were protected in the 1920s, when they switched to the eggs of guillemots and terns. Eiders were also shot in large numbers for meat, as well as being killed for their down. Eider down has excellent insulation qualities. It has been collected and exported from Greenland and Iceland to Denmark and other markets in large quantities. After over-exploitation in the 19th century the ducks were legally protected in the mid-20th century and numbers have recovered; though the farming of down is still pursued in Greenland, for instance, where the

Drake common eider

annual harvest comes from some 100,000 nests, and from Iceland, with an annual take of some 150,000 nests. Traditionally the Inuit in Greenland made shirts from the skins of the ducks, needing 15–20 skins for one shirt – new shirts were made annually. A hundred skins made a rug, a trade only stopped in Denmark in 1939. The Canadian Inuit used the skins to make blankets.

Eiders are coastal diving ducks, depending on a supply of littoral crustaceans and molluscs to nourish them. It has been calculated that on the Murman coast of the Barents Sea 1,500 eiders breeding on seven islands there took 60 tonnes of molluscs in a summer.

They move south to moult in July and August, then winter at the edge of a polynya. Cold winters may occasion much mortality, especially if weak tidal movements allow the water to freeze, denying access to the diving grounds. These conditions may well also encourage snowy owls to take advantage of weakened and easy prey.

Eider incubation lasts about four weeks, with the female doing all the work. The drake leaves her to it after a couple of weeks of protection, when he gathers in a sociable flock with other males. On hatching, the duck leads the ducklings to the sea, where they join with others in large nurseries; the female then moults and fattens for the southward migration. They are not above diving for the molluscs at a mussel farm, presumably arguing that they were fishing there before the farmer arrived.

The familiar name 'cuddy duck' comes from the association with St Cuthbert, an early saint who offered the ducks sanctuary on the Farne Islands off the Northumberland coast of England, where he established the first nature reserve in the world. He had a special affection for eiders which thus, in the 7th century, became the first birds in the world to be given formal protection.

KING EIDER
Somateria spectabilis

King eiders are common in the North Pacific, decidedly less common in the Arctic Ocean, and least common of all in Iceland and northern Scandinavia. The males have a striking orange frontal shield on the bill, bordered with black. The females look confusingly similar to those of the common eider.

Less colonial than the common eider, they scatter nests around small tundra ponds in a small hollow scraped in the open, sometimes in the lee of a rock or rise. Four or five eggs are laid in June; incubation takes 22–4 days. The drakes leave the incubating ducks after a few days to join clubs of moulting males. Fledging period for the ducklings is not known. They leave the nest soon after hatching to follow the duck in foraging. Main food is found by diving close inshore for molluscs and crustaceans, plus insect larvae and other marine invertebrates. They eat some tundra vegetation.

The small Svalbard population probably migrates south to winter along the coast of northern Norway, but they are seldom seen below the Arctic Circle. They are common at sea outside the breeding season. The greatest numbers of post-breeding moulting king eiders gather off the central west coast of Greenland. Perhaps as many as 100,000 drakes and immature birds may be found in the Davis Strait in late summer.

*Length
45–63cm
(19–26in)*

*Wingspan
86–102cm
(36–43in)*

The duck is easily confused with a common eider.

RAPTORS

Raptors – birds of prey – are diurnal carnivores, hunting live prey, though they are not above taking carrion. Typically they have strong feet with which they grab and kill, while powerful hooked bills are used for tearing prey. The males are usually smaller than females. They are superb fliers.

WHITE-TAILED SEA-EAGLE
Haliaeetus albicilla

Length
70–90cm (28–35in)

Wingspan
200–240cm
(79–94in)

The white-tailed sea-eagle is a large, vulture-like eagle with a huge bill and long neck. It appears massive in flight, with broad, rectangular, deeply fingered wings and a white wedge-shaped tail. It is fairly widespread along the coasts of the Russian Arctic,

Scandinavia (but not Svalbard), Iceland and southwest Greenland (as well as the Middle East and Eurasia).

There are perhaps a hundred pairs in the sheep-rearing southwest of Greenland, where they breed north to 67°, and perhaps ten breeding pairs on the west coast of Iceland.

These sea-eagles show a preference for small islands and skerries in sheltered waters with plenty of fish. Eyries are often built on the highest point of low outlying skerries, rarely on the ground, never high up. They have several nests, used in rotation. They are bulky structures built by both sexes from birch and willow twigs and branches, several feet high, lined with an egg-cup of mosses and lichens and greenery. One to four eggs are laid in May, incubated by both parents for 38–45 days. Once hatched the male does most of the hunting while the female guards the nest and chicks. Chicks need 800gm of fish daily.

Ninety percent of the prey items are fish, for instance dogfish and lumpsuckers; the other 10% consists of birds and the odd fox. Diving ducks like eiders, also auks, are harassed by the eagle which, in forcing them to dive continuously, weakens them till they are easy prey. They also take gulls.

The species was once widespread in Europe, but suffered persecution on account of its supposed predation on lambs. In real life it seems likely that, although they occasionally took advantage of a sick or newborn lamb, this has never been a significant activity. Stories of young babies carried off by sea eagles were part of the folklore of remote areas, but there has never been much evidence.

Populations of the white-tailed sea-eagle declined throughout the 20th century. Since 1973 they have been fully protected by law in Greenland, but they still succumb to fox traps and are shot for stuffing as glass-case specimens. Re-introductions to the Hebrides are slowly establishing a British breeding presence there.

'It is impossible to conceal the fact that if the present destruction of eagles continues we shall have to reckon this species among the extinct families of our feathered nobility.'
R Gray, 1871

Sea-eagle, from an 8th-century manuscript, Corpus Christi collection, Cambridge. In medieval times the eagle symbolised the evangelist St John, but subsequently it suffered greatly, persecuted as 'vermin'.

GYRFALCON
Falco rusticolus

Length
50–60cm
(21–25in)

Wingspan
130–160cm
(54–67in)

A truly Arctic species, the gyrfalcon is circumpolar and the most northerly of breeding falcons. A coastal and inshore bird, it holds vast territories. The female, known as the falcon, is somewhat larger than the male, known as the tiercel, but both are big. Colour and size vary from dark grey-brown to white with the white ones being on average slightly larger.

In fact they are trimorphic, with three distinct colour phases, or morphs. The white phase occurs most commonly in the north of the range, where the birds tend to be slightly larger. Gyrfalcons are widely distributed around the Arctic coast, penetrating south even to the trees at the edge of the Alaskan taiga. They are rare in Svalbard, probably because of the shortage of lemmings, but are particularly well established around the coast of Greenland.

Dark phase of gyrfalcon; more typical of the southern end of the range

Gyrfalcons breed on ledges on cliff crags, tucked in under an overhang, in a mountainous habitat, starting their cycle while conditions are still wintry. They may take over the nest of another species, for instance that of a raven, but they do little in the way of improving it.

A slight scrape serves their purpose. Three to five reddish brown eggs are laid in April or May on top of the historic deposit of guano. The tiercel brings courtship food offerings and continues to supply the falcon at the nest till the chicks fledge. Incubation is five weeks; fledging takes seven weeks.

The principal prey is ptarmigan and willow grouse, but they may also take lemmings and hares. Closer to the coast they will prey on auks, gulls and terns. In autumn they will take advantage of flocks of small migrating birds, such as buntings. They hunt fast and low in sparrowhawk fashion, taking birds by surprise or by aerial stoop, when they break the neck or tear the head off the prey.

Greenland gyrfalcons migrate south within Greenland for the winter, though many of the white-phase Greenlandic birds make for Iceland. However, individuals may turn up in the Faroes or in the British Isles. Most birds winter north of 52° whether on the American or European side of the Atlantic.

Many thousands of eyasses (fledglings) have been taken from the nest in the past, originally for falconry but also for museum specimens. Much prized through the ages by falconers, and reserved for kings and emperors, they were taken as early as the 14th century from the Baltic coast for the European aristocracy. Medieval Norwegian kings presented them as prestige gifts to high-ranking diplomats, foreign monarchs and popes. They were trapped by skilled Dutchmen who learnt their trade at home catching peregrines on passage. From the 17th century the Dutchmen were to be found in Iceland, using ptarmigans instead of pigeons as tethered decoys. They are now fully protected in law, though some are still said to be taken illegally in the interest of certain Middle Eastern potentates. The white morph, which is usually larger than the grey, is greatly prized for falconry. The primary feathers have been used for arrows and spears by Alaskan Eskimos, and they have been used as barter in trading with coastal Inuit, in areas where gyrfalcons were rare. The species is also bred in captivity for the benefit of legal followers of the sport.

Gyrfalcon nests occupy traditional sites. The accumulation of guano may be almost 2m deep. At one active nest carbon-dating has shown that the bottom layers were deposited 2,500 years ago.

In medieval times gyrfalcons were highly prized. Marco Polo wrote of their mysterious origin on an island 'in the northern ocean'. Kubla Khan travelled 'attended by full ten thousand falconers, with gyr falcons, peregrines and sakers'.

PEREGRINE FALCON

Falco peregrinus

*Length
36–48cm
(15–20in)*

*Wingspan
95–110cm
(40–46in)*

A stocky falcon with a short tail and a prominent 'moustache', the peregrine is compact and powerful. In flight its wings are broadly based but sharply tapered towards the tips. The female is significantly larger than the male. It is widely distributed, from the tropics to the Arctic, where it is circumpolar, with strongholds in Novaya Zemlya, Franz Josef Land and the Siberian Arctic. Smaller than the gyrfalcon, it does not penetrate so far north and has totally different hunting habits. Well established in the southern half of Greenland, where it nests as far north as Upernavik on the west coast and Ammassalik on the east, there are as many as 70 young produced annually from some 22 cliff sites. It is not recorded in Iceland or Svalbard.

The name 'peregrine' means 'wanderer' and it is especially true of those breeding in the Arctic that they migrate great distances to avoid the harsh winter.

Peregrine falcons tend to occupy the same hunting territory every year on their return in May to the breeding grounds, but may well choose a new nest site. They make a mere scrape on a convenient cliff ledge and lay three to four eggs. The Greenland population was less affected than the others by the catastrophic declines of the 1950s and 1960s, when one of the effects of agricultural pesticides was to cause peregrines to produce eggshells so thin that they broke easily in the nest. The eggs are incubated for 29–32 days, with fledging occuring at 35–42 days. The chicks are heavily dependent on their parents for a couple of months, brooded by the female while the male hunts and provides most of the food in the early days of parenthood. If lemmings are available, they will take them, but prey is mainly small birds, mostly snow and Lapland buntings, but some redpolls and wheatears. Young birds learn their trade by attacking flying insects before they graduate to sterner prey.

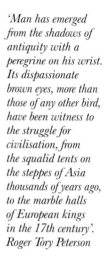

The peregrine hunting technique differs profoundly from that of the gyrfalcon, which hunts in the same territory, but in the manner of a sparrowhawk, fast and low. In the case of the peregrine, it is a sensational performance in which the soaring bird stoops from a great height – almost vertically and at great speed – on to its prey in a partially closed-wing power dive which may reach a speed of over 200mph and actually makes a howling noise – it must be the last thing a bunting hears before it is knocked senseless.

Peregrine falcons move south for the winter. They have suffered greatly from the activities of egg collectors and those who trap live specimens for falconry.

'Man has emerged from the shadows of antiquity with a peregrine on his wrist. Its dispassionate brown eyes, more than those of any other bird, have been witness to the struggle for civilisation, from the squalid tents on the steppes of Asia thousands of years ago, to the marble halls of European kings in the 17th century'.
Roger Tory Peterson

PURPLE SANDPIPER

Calidris maritima

Length
20–22cm
(8–9in)

Wingspan
42–46cm
(18–19in)

With its slaty breeding plumage and longish bill, while in the Arctic the purple sandpiper resembles a dark dunlin but lacks the black belly. Its short legs are a distinctive orangey-yellow in its more southerly winter quarters, but in the north they are greyish-brown. While it may not be colourful, the purple sandpiper makes itself known as it fusses about looking for titbits. Markedly tame and confiding, gregarious by nature, it is a rather portly bird.

These birds are common coastal breeders throughout the Arctic coast and islands, from Canada to Siberia, from sea level to 300m. They are well established and common around the south coast of Greenland, the whole of Iceland and the west coast of Spitsbergen. Less common at Franz Josef Land.

While they sometimes choose sites on shingle beaches and coastal lagoons, most purple sandpipers nest on wet tundra where there is plenty of vegetation. The male excavates a series of small cups and the female makes the choice of the one which is to receive the three or four eggs in June. It seems that the male does most of the incubating, which takes 21–2 days. Chicks leave the nest soon after hatching, and while they are cared for by both parents at first, the female slopes off after a couple of weeks, leaving the male to take full responsibility for care of the brood.

Food is found mostly from marshy pools and from rock crevices: invertebrates mainly, but also some vegetation, including buds, berries and seeds. Along the shore they turn seaweed in the manner of a turnstone. In soil they jab and probe for insects such as craneflies and midges. In hunting they parade busily around the edge of a pond.

In due course, the parent male and the offspring follow the female to the shore, where numbers of sandpipers congregate to moult before the southward migration in August or September. They fly far enough to escape the ice, to southwest Greenland, to Iceland and western Norway and south to the British Isles and the Atlantic coast, always bound for rocky shores.

OTHER ARCTIC WADERS
Too many species of waders take advantage of the short but insect-productive Arctic summer to be dealt with in this book. They are mostly tundra-breeders. The purple sandpiper and grey phalarope are the ones most likely to be seen by a visitor to the coast, though turnstones, *Arenaria interpres*, are fairly common feeding along beaches and nesting on rocky islands. Some of the waders (shorebirds) make astonishing migratory journeys to take advantage of the short but cornucopian 24 hours of summer daylight. Some of the sandpipers and sanderlings come from the south of South America, covering more than 14,000km: the journey compares well with the world-beating flights of the Arctic tern, which breeds in the high Arctic and 'winters' in the Antarctic Weddell Sea, living a life of perpetual summer.

GREY PHALAROPE
(Red phalarope)
Phalaropus fulicarius

Length
20–22cm
(8–9in)

Wingspan
40–44cm
(17–18in)

Of the three species of phalarope, the grey (known confusingly as the red in North America) is the most marine – the shorebird most likely to be seen by coastal visitors in the breeding season. It is superbly adapted to aquatic life, with lobed webs on its toes, as in the unrelated grebes. It is a fearless bird, surprisingly indifferent to human approach. Yet another surprise is that the female is larger and much more colourful than the male. In breeding plumage the female has a white face with a dark crown and yellow beak, its upperparts are boldly patterned, its underparts a striking dark chestnut. The male is dowdy by comparison, an indication of the atypical breeding strategy of this species, where traditional rôles are reversed and the female is the dominant partner in courtship and copulation. However, she cannot escape responsibility for laying the eggs.

Grey phalaropes are circumpolar in distribution, common in summer along the high and low Arctic coast. On arrival in May or early June they wait at the edge of the sea ice for the thaw to reveal the ground on the nesting areas. At this time they have empty stomachs after the long haul of migration and are quick to take advantage of the burgeoning insect life of pools, shallow inshore waters and tideline.

They are loosely colonial and non-territorial at the breeding grounds, the season starting in early June in Iceland and Svalbard, later in Arctic Russia. The chosen sites are on marshy tundra or small islands in country with plenty of freshwater ponds with abundant vegetation. Both sexes make several nests, forming neat cups, with available materials, always close to water. The female makes the final choice. Courtship is initiated by the female and the pair bond lasts just long enough for her to provide her mate with a clutch of three or four eggs, which it then becomes his job to incubate. The female promptly abandons him to join a club of other females and non-breeders of both sexes off the coast (although on occasion she might take the opportunity of mating and providing another male with a clutch to incubate).

Phalaropes sometimes congregate to take advantage of the oily secretions of whales or take parasites from a whale's back. In past times, flocks led whalers to their prey.

Incubation, for 18–20 days, is entirely the responsibility of the male, who, in order to be inconspicuous at the nest, has suitably dowdy plumage. He starts incubation when the last egg has been laid by the female before she departs, so the chicks are born more-or-less simultaneously. Vulnerable to predation at the nest, they leave without delay, in the care of the male.

Grey phalaropes feed on insect larvae and other small aquatic organisms, wading at the edge of the pool or swimming in tight circles like a spinning top, to encourage food items to the surface, where they are picked off daintily with the thin, pointed bill. As soon as the young can fly, the family party goes to sea.

Females migrate south in mid-July, the males with their brood follow later. The most oceanic of the phalaropes, they move from the polar breeding grounds far south to winter at sea on the plankton-rich waters off West Africa and eastern South America. Insubstantial birds they may seem, but in fact they happily endure rough seas, riding high in the water.

The closely related red-necked phalarope P. lobatus is smaller and slimmer, with fewer red underparts and with a more boldly patterned back. Both are adept at spin-stirring prey items on freshwater ponds. Both winter below the equator.

SKUAS

The name 'skua' comes from the Icelandic *skufr* and is presumably a rendering of their chase-call in flight. Known to North Americans as *jaegers*, skuas are large, gull-like seabirds with dark plumage and markedly angled wings. They have conspicuous white patches at the base of the primaries. Superficially like immature gulls, they are heavier, more robust and menacing in mien, as befits a bird of prey. Theirs is a piratical nature and they have hawk-like beaks to serve it. They are kleptoparasites – carnivorous buccaneers – chasing other birds, mostly gulls and terns, in the air and forcing them to disgorge their catch. True seabirds, they come ashore only to breed.

POMARINE SKUA
(Pomarine jaeger)
Stercorarius pomarinus

*...chasing a
juvenile kittiwake*

*Length
46–51cm
(19–21in)*

*Wingspan
125–138cm
(52–58in)*

'Pomarine' is the shortened form of 'pomatorhine' – lid-nosed – which derives from the nostrils being partly covered by a scale. That description actually applies equally to all the skuas, and distinguishes them from the gulls, but time has given the corrupted form of the name only to this particular species.

This bird is smaller than the great skua but larger than the other long-tailed skuas, and decorated with strikingly long, blunt and spoon-shaped twisted tail feathers. Both sexes look alike, with a dark crown and golden yellow sides to the head. It is polymorphic, in two colour phases, either all-brown or brown with white underparts. The lighter phase outnumbers the dark by twenty to one. A thickset and powerful bird, its flight is slow and purposeful with steady wing beats. It is often seen following ships, especially trawlers.

Pomarine skua tail

The pomarine skua is circumpolar on the Arctic coastal tundra, preferring low-lying areas with freshwater pools. It is not common in Greenland or Svalbard.

Both sexes choose the nest site and make an insubstantial ground nest – a shallow scrape, if anything, with possibly a few scraps of moss or vegetation. Two eggs are laid, incubated by both parents for 23–8 days. Chicks usually leave the nest after a few days but stay in the area. They are fed by regurgitation. The chicks fledge in about five weeks but are dependent on their parents for a couple more weeks before they are able to fly independently.

At nesting time the abundance of lemmings is a prime factor in breeding success. In a poor lemming year skuas may choose not to attempt breeding. As a food substitute they will also take eggs and young of other birds.

When the breeding season is over, towards the end of September and somewhat later than other skuas, travelling partly overland, they leave the tundra, making for the open sea around the equator in both the Atlantic and the Pacific. Now they are ocean wanderers, specialising in areas of strong upwellings with their abundant surface life. They fish by dipping to grab from the surface. They can be adventurous in soliciting handouts: I offered cruise-ship buns and had them taking food from the hand while far out at sea in the North Pacific.

ARCTIC SKUA

(Parasitic skua, parasitic jaeger, Richardson's skua)
Stercorarius parasiticus

Length
41–46cm
(17–19in)

Wingspan
110–125cm
(46–52in)

As with the pomarine, the Arctic skua is also polymorphic, with two colour phases, light and dark – the lighter form having a dark breast band and becoming commoner further north. Its main distinguishing feature is the central tail streamer, which is shorter than that of the long-tailed skua. Arctic skuas have been seen only a few miles short of the North Pole, and have been known to call at remote camps on the Greenland ice-cap to beg for scraps. Smaller than the great skua and the pomarine, they are the commonest skuas of the west Palearctic, circumpolar in distribution, from well above 80° down to 57°N. They are common in Greenland and on the west and north coast of Spitsbergen.

Arctic skuas breed on barren coasts and islands. Usually found in single pairs but sometimes in loose colonies, in close association with auk or kittiwake or tern colonies, since these provide abundant food in the form of half-fledged chicks at a convenient time in the nesting cycle. They prefer a dry nest site amid swampy ground. The pair bond is strong, probably for life. They usually breed first in their fourth year. Commonly two eggs are laid in June, and are incubated by both sexes for 24–8 days. The young leave the nest soon after hatching, and are fed by both parents. They defend their nest territory vigorously, intruders being dealt with by a graded sequence of reactions, depending on the perceived danger. They perform a distraction display in which one bird feigns injury – a wing drooping pathetically as it 'struggles' to lure the intruder, perhaps a man or a fox, away from the nest or chicks. The bird stumbles along the ground, squealing and holding out a 'broken' wing, only to take off and fly away boldly once the intruder is at a safe distance. If the interloper goes closer to the nest or chicks the intensity of the display is doubled, and the other parent will stoop from the air in a powerful attack, even tearing a person's scalp and causing bleeding. Always do what the bird asks, i.e. walk towards it and therefore away from the chicks it is protecting.

Arctic skua tail

Both parents care for the young until well after fledging. The young birds fly in about four to five weeks, fed well on a diet of the half-fledged auks, terns and kittiwakes whose colonies are nearby and provide easy pickings.

Outside the breeding season, Arctic skuas are fast piratical predators, forcing gulls and terns to throw up their fish catch. They winter at sea off the coasts of the southern hemisphere.

LONG-TAILED SKUA

(Long-tailed jaeger)

Stercorarius longicaudus

Length
48–53cm
(20–22in)

Wingspan
105–117cm
(44–49in)

Distribution of the long-tailed skua is circumpolar in the Arctic tundra from northern Canada by way of Greenland, Iceland, Svalbard and the coast of Siberia. Long-tailed skuas look like a smaller and less robust version of the pale phase Arctic skua, with extremely long and slender tail feathers, which may appear as long as the rest of the body. The crown is a more clear-cut black than the Arctic skua, and the breeding adult lacks the breast band. There is a dark phase version but it is very rare. Flight is more graceful and buoyant than that of the Arctic skua.

They arrive at the breeding grounds in May, settling in loose-knit colonies on high tundra and scree. Pairs form soon after arrival. Each territory contains a lookout point located on a hummock or something similar. The nest is in a shallow depression on the ground, perhaps on a raised peat mound or amongst stony scree. Long-tailed skuas are less enthusiastic for small islands and skerries, often well inland. The nest is usually unlined.

Two eggs are laid in June or early July. Both parents incubate, but the male does most of the hunting, bringing prey to the female on the nest where he skins and tears it apart and shares the food. The incubation period is 23–5 days. Breeding success is dependent on a healthy population of lemmings and other small mammals, though they have been known to take advantage of fish refuse and offal at a human camp. The female does most of the brooding and feeding of the chicks, while the male hunts and defends the territory. Two days after hatching, the chicks leave the nest to hide in vegetation, running to the parents when they fly in with food. After a week or two they begin to tear their own morsels. Fledging takes 24–6 days. Their main prey is lemmings and other small mammals, forming 90% of the diet, topped up with birds, fish, insects and even berries.

Long-tailed skua tail

Both adults tend the chicks for about three weeks after fledging, when they all leave the breeding grounds. The chicks will not return until they breed in their third summer.

Like the Arctic skua, long-tailed skuas are pelagic outside the breeding season, but they winter even further south, in southern Africa, South America and the Southern Ocean.

GREAT SKUA
(Bonxie)
Stercorarius skua

Length
53–58cm
(22–24in)

Wingspan
132–140cm
(55–58in)

Bonxie - the name universally used by birders – probably comes from the Norse 'bunki', when in Shetlandese it became 'bunksi' – dumpy and untidy. The great skua is indeed like a big stocky herring gull, but dark brown all over, with conspicuous tell-tale white flashes on the wings and a short tail. Its flight is heavy and rather laboured, except when it is engaged in piracy, when it chases fish-loaded birds with relentless purpose, agility and speed, forcing them to disgorge or drop their catch.

The most widely distributed of the skuas (its very close relative the Antarctic brown skua breeds in the high southern latitudes) the great skua is the least common of the four skuas in the Arctic. Nevertheless, it has a foothold of sorts from Greenland to Finnmark along Arctic coasts, though it is much more common further south. Established for a long time in Iceland

and northern Britain, it extended its range both north and south in the 20th century, breeding now on Bear Island and Svalbard (not uncommon on the west coast of Spitsbergen).

Great skuas return to the Arctic breeding grounds in late May. They are fond of communal bathing in fresh water. Sometimes seen as a lone pair and sometimes in a small colony often with many non-breeders in the vicinity, great skuas defend their territory with vigour. Their chosen site is mostly on upland tundra close to rocky coast. There is always a convenient lookout which serves as a loafing or roosting site. The nest is made as soon as the snow melts – a meagre scrape with scant lining. Both sexes, but mostly the female, incubate the two eggs, laid in early June, for 28–30 days. The parents are aggressive in defence of the nest and chicks and will dive-bomb and physically attack an intruder, whether fox or human, giving a glancing blow with the feet which are lowered at the last moment as the bird attacks from behind. They often draw blood from a scalp wound.

Great skua tail

In the breeding season, piracy is less evident, with other birds and eggs becoming an important item of prey, gathered from a hunting territory which is distinct from that for breeding. The chicks leave the nest two or three days after hatching, to hide in nearby vegetation and wait for feeding visits by the parents, when they run out to beg vociferously. The young are assiduously cared for by both parents, fledge in six to seven weeks, soon become independent and leave the breeding area to go to the sea. It is here that they learn the trade of a pirate, harrying terns, gulls and even gannets to relieve them of their catch. Great skuas will also take advantage of carrion and commonly follow ships, especially if they are fishing.

Great skuas are pelagic in winter, from the Bay of Biscay and south to the waters off West Africa and west to the Newfoundland Banks and Brazil.

GULLS

Gulls are sturdy and sociable birds with powerful bills, webbed feet, long and pointed bow-shaped wings and fairly short, square tails. The sexes are similar in plumage, immatures tending to a mottled grey-brown, adults becoming more white, grey and black after several years. They nest noisily and colonially, sometimes in large numbers, often in close proximity to a convenient food source. Scavengers by trade, they take anything from seashore invertebrates to carrion to the eggs and chicks of other birds, including those of their own species.

ICELAND GULL

Larus glaucoides

Length 52–60cm (22–25in)
Wingspan 140–150cm (58–63in)

Confined to the North Atlantic, the nominate species breeds only in Greenland, mainly on the west coast, while the sub-species *L. g. kumlieni* breeds on Baffin Island and northwest Quebec. As names go, it does seem an eccentric one, but is almost justified by the fact that the Greenland birds at least winter in northern Iceland.

This gull has translucent white tips to the primaries, a pale grey mantle, white head and a yellow bill with a red spot. It is smaller and less robust than the similar-looking and much commoner glaucous gull. Its flight may seem quicker in action and more buoyant than the glaucous and in flight the general whiteness is marked.

In the breeding season they frequent low-Arctic rocky coasts, but usually well away from the open sea, preferring fjords and sheltered waters. They return to the breeding grounds in late April or May, nesting on generous ledges on skerries, stacks and high steep cliffs. They are sometimes associated with kittiwake colonies, which may occur well in from the open sea alongside glacier faces.

They feed mainly on fish taken by inshore plunge-diving, but will also scavenge to take advantage of tideline carrion like dead fish and birds; they also take the eggs and young of other birds, though not to the extent indulged in by glaucous gulls.

Post-breeding, Canadian birds winter on the west Atlantic coast south to New England; West Greenland birds move to the coast in August, dispersing between Thule in the north and Nuuk in the south. Birds from the east Greenland population tend to winter on the north coast of Iceland. Vagrants show up in northern Europe.

SALTY PROBLEMS
Divers, gulls and seabirds in general have a particular problem when it comes to dealing with the quantity of salt which they inevitably ingest in both drinking and fishing. They absorb far more than is healthy for them and more than their renal system can deal with. The surplus salt is conveyed by a network of blood vessels into fine tubes connected with the nasal glands. This concentrated sodium chloride turns into a solution and drips constantly from the end of the beak.

SABINE'S GULL
Larus sabini

*Length
27–32cm
(11–13in)*

*Wingspan
90–100cm
(38–42in)*

A truly Arctic bird, Sabine's gull is circumpolar in the sub- and high Arctic. It is less common in the Atlantic sector of the Arctic, and moderately well established in Greenland. A few, possibly pioneers originating from Greenland, breed on Moffen Island and the west coast of Spitsbergen, probably none on Franz Josef Land.

Sabine's gull is a graceful bird, smaller than the kittiwake, and roughly the size of an Arctic tern. It is light and agile in flight and can be identified by its black hood, black bill with yellow tip and white forked tail. In flight, the upperwing shows a conspicuous white triangle contrasted with black primaries. The dark grey mantle completes a strikingly M-shaped pattern. This tri-coloured upper wing has similarities with the M-pattern on the juvenile kittiwake's wing but Sabine's is smaller and has longer, narrower wings. It is also more buoyant in flight than the kittiwake. There may be possible confusion with the juvenile Ross's gull, but both Sabine's and Ross's are decidedly uncommon by comparison with kittiwakes.

These gulls return to the colony in May or June, making for well-vegetated coastal lowlands, islets and islands, always close to the sea. Usually they are in close association with Arctic tern colonies, taking advantage of the protection from predators provided by the aggressive terns, which harry any intruder unmercifully (though the gulls are no slouches when it comes to aggression).

In marshy tundra or by brackish ponds with grassy-mossy edges, they make an unlined shallow scrape in the open, depositing two eggs in June. Incubation is by both parents for 23–5 days. The young leave the nest a day or so after hatching, to follow their parents to the nearest water, where they very soon learn to feed themselves. Insects are the most important item of diet at this stage, but larvae, crustaceans, worms, snails and small fishes are all grist to the mill. They soon learn to hover and dip for food, much in the manner of the terns they share space with.

At the end of the breeding season, in late August or September, they migrate south to a life at sea. Both the Canadian and Greenlandic birds, together with those few from Spitsbergen and the Russian coast, winter south of the equator, in Atlantic waters off South Africa, after passing by way of the northwest European coast.

EDWARD SABINE

Sabine's gull was discovered by Edward Sabine in 1818, on islands which now bear his name – Sabineøer – south of Thule in west Greenland. Sabine was the naturalist with Captain John Ross RN (uncle of James Clark Ross) when he was exploring the northern part of the Davis Strait in search of the elusive Northwest Passage with HMS *Isabella* and HMS *Alexander*. In Melville Bay he shot and took specimens of an 'elegant forktailed gull – hitherto unknown and undescribed' – from a mixed colony of gulls and terns.

GLAUCOUS GULL

Larus hyperboreus

*Length
62–68cm
(26–28in)*

*Wingspan
150–165cm
(63–69in)*

'Glaucous' is from the Greek *glaukos*, meaning 'bright or gleaming'. This species is circumpolar, coastal and common from northeast Canada, Greenland, Iceland, Svalbard and Siberia. It is larger than a herring gull and has an aggressive character. Its upperparts are pale grey with white wingtips. Its head is heavy with a large bill and a glowering expression and its body looks very solid.

Glaucous gulls breed in the high Arctic but also on sub-Arctic coasts. They favour islands, lagoons and sea cliffs, especially if set back from the shore by a stretch of rough pasture. Often found near settlements and in association with barnacle goose grounds, kittiwake or auk colonies which provide convenient prey. In Svalbard, they are sometimes seen as lone pairs or in small colonies, but again near colonies of other birds. They will visit ships in the hope of scraps, perching fearlessly on the rails.

Both sexes build the nest – a bulky pile of seaweed plus a certain amount of available vegetation, lined perhaps with a few feathers. Usually it is placed on a rocky outcrop, cliff edge or cliff slope. Two or three eggs are laid in late May or early June, incubated by both birds for 27–8 days. The chicks leave the nest a day or two after hatching, with both parents who care for them. Fledging may be 45–50 days, after which the young are soon independent.

Unlike most seabirds, glaucous gulls find a proportion of their food on land, though they will also take molluscs from the shore. They are omnivorous but in the breeding season they sustain themselves mostly from the eggs and chicks of other birds. As piratical scavengers they take eggs and young of auks and kittiwakes from their cliff ledges. Waiting below the cliff face, they take young birds as they make their first perilous flight from the nest ledge and also lie in wait for those chicks which have to run the gauntlet from the cliff base over tundra to the sea. The gulls also rob eider and fulmar nests for eggs and chicks. Storm-tossed mussels may be taken on the beach, where they will also search for fly larvae in decaying weed. Seal faeces may provide some nourishment. (In the Pacific Bering Sea, they may feed on the detritus brought to the surface by bottom-feeding grey whales.) Little auks are eaten whole.

As a consequence of feeding on the chicks and eggs of other birds like the auks, glaucous gulls have endured a high level of PCB pollutants, but fortunately PCB and DDT levels in, for instance, Barents Sea seabirds, have been decreasing over the last decade.

Birds from the Canadian Arctic and west Greenland are either resident or migrate south into eastern North America. The relatively smaller east Greenland population winters in Iceland. Svalbard birds drop down to Norway and the Faroes, some remaining in open water areas of the Barents Sea, some even reaching as far south as the British Isles.

ROSS'S GULL
Rhodostethia rosea

Length
29–31cm
(12–13in)

Wingspan
90–100cm
(38–42in)

A small gull, Ross's gull resembles the little gull *Larus minutus* in many respects, but with a black necklace and underparts suffused a delicate pink; it is the only gull with a wedge-shaped tail. It is lusted after by every birder, mainly because of its reclusive rarity but also on account of its delicate beauty and its graceful movements both on the ground and in flight.

The bird was first described as the 'collared gull' by virtue of the necklace, but the honour of first describing it later went to the Royal Navy. It was in June 1823, when midshipman James Clark Ross was ship's naturalist with HMS *Hecla*, searching for the elusive Northwest Passage, that another midshipman, William Parry, recorded in the expedition's journal:

'Our shooting parties have of late been tolerably successful. Mr Ross procured a specimen of gull having a black ring round its neck, and which in its present plumage, we could not find described.'

The collared gull soon became Ross's rosy gull but finally Ross's gull.

It is not clear whether the delicate shell-pink breast colour comes from a diet of shrimps or from a pigment in the preen oil which is extracted from the bird's tail gland. The colour persists even in winter, but is most intense at courtship time. The breeding grounds of this gull were one of the great mysteries of the ornithological world until early in the twentieth century. It is a truly Arctic bird, breeding only rarely south of the Arctic Circle. Very few breed successfully between Svalbard and eastern Canada, a few on low islets in the Resolute area on the south coast of Cornwallis Island in the Canadian Arctic, and a few in north and west Greenland. The main area is around the deltas of the north Siberian rivers, in fact every river delta between the Chukchi and Taimyr peninsulas. There they nest on islands in lakes and on tundra swamps some 200 miles north of the Arctic Circle, not far north of the tree zone. At the breeding grounds on the tundra of the Vilkitsky Islands I have seen them swimming and paddling over marshy pools, picking off fly larvae and sundry insects, astonishingly tame and almost indifferent to human approach. Those breeding around Pokholdst on the Kolyna River at about 69° north are said to migrate *on foot*, with young which are still in an unfledged downy state, in order to reach the shores of the Arctic and its plentiful food. On the water's surface, they may pick insects in the manner of a phalarope, hovering like a tern or plunge-diving like a kittiwake.

In the summer it is possible to see fair numbers of non-breeders in summer plumage north of east Svalbard (Nordauslandet) and Franz Josef Land, as well as along the edge of the fast ice between Svalbard and north Greenland in the north Norwegian Sea.

The least known of all gulls, Ross's gull's life is closely associated with ice and the feeding possibilities it

HMS Hecla

Sir James Clark Ross was distinguished both as navigator and scientist. As commander of the British Antarctic Expedition of 1839–43 with Erebus *and* Terror *he discovered the last known and least known of all pinnipeds, Ross's seal (Ommatophoca rossii).*

provides – the algae which thrive on the underside of the floes. But something of a mystery still remains of its migrations as its winter whereabouts are unknown. In autumn it is regularly seen on passage in northwesterly gales off Point Barrow in Alaska: unlikely as it may seem, it heads in a northeasterly direction, towards the polar pack-ice. Yet it is not seen on any return passage in spring, so where do the birds winter? It has been surmised that they remain in the high Arctic, around the edges of the pack or by polynyas offering open water, north of the breeding grounds, but recent research points to the probability that winter is spent far out at sea somewhere south of the Bering Sea in the north Pacific, some 1,000 miles from its breeding areas.

Until well into the 20th century the Eskimos of Point Barrow in northern Alaska shot Ross's gulls for the pot as they passed on their autumn migration.

'My plumage bears
the crimson blush
When ocean by the
sun is kissed.'
Longfellow

'I did get a good crack at the Ross Gulls again this fall [1928]. One day, the 26th of September, they were around in thousands. If I could have had time, I could have had several hundred birds to skin. The Eskimo shoot them for food, and they are mighty good at that. I have eaten them many times, and this fall I had them fried and roasted until I almost turned into a Ross Gull myself. They taste just as do the golden plover, and are just as fat in the fall.'

Collector Charles D Brower,
reporting on his prowess to the
San Diego Society of Natural History,
in the journal *Condor*, 1929

BLACK-LEGGED KITTIWAKE
Rissa tridactyla

Although the kittiwake is an ocean-going gull, in the breeding season its habitat is low and high Arctic coast as far north as there is open water for fishing. It will even nest on glacier ledges or the face of a snowbank if there are no ice-free ledges. Arctic Canada, Greenland, Iceland, Bear Island, Svalbard and the Bering Sea are all colonised (as well as the coast of northwest Europe).

It has a slender lemony-yellow bill, short black legs and a demure black eye which gives it a less loutish appearance than most gulls. The flight is buoyant and bounding, with a shallow wing beat. There are no white tips to the wings, which have 'dipped in ink' ends. Its call is a pleasantly onomatopoeic 'kitty-wa-ake'.

Kittiwakes enjoy a strong pair bond and are colonial nesters, from a couple of dozen pairs to a seabird city

Length
38–40cm
(16–17in)

Wingspan
95–120cm
(40–50in)

of thousands, often in the company of Brünnich's guillemots in the Arctic. They build cantilevered nests, sometimes on the narrowest ledges of very steep sea-cliffs and caves, places which offer maximum protection from marauding foxes. Where there are settlements, they may nest on window ledges. In fishing-boat harbours they will nest on the tractor tyres used as fenders on the wharves. Typically they cluster in large numbers near the snouts of glaciers, where a constant run-off of fresh water collides with the slightly warmer sea. The result is accelerated plankton production. When great chunks of ice calve from the snout, clouds of kittiwakes gather at the disturbed water to pick off the tiny crustaceans, eg: *Thyannoessa inermis* which crowd the surface. They also enjoy communal flights to a freshwater pond to bathe.

The nest is carefully constructed and compacted of seaweed, mud and grasses, plastered on narrow ledges. Usually two eggs are laid in late May or June; incubation is by both sexes for 26–8 days. The newborn chicks are programmed to sit very still, for if they were to walk about they would be in danger of falling from a great height to a certain death. (Most gulls leave their ground nests – dangerous places – a couple of days after hatching, to lie camouflaged in the greenery while their parents forage for food.) The chicks are fed by both parents. Feeding is by regurgitation, an adaptation to the confined space which requires them to sit tight, until they fly at about six weeks. The birds defecate carefully over the edge of the nest, so that there are conspicuous patches of white below, encouraging a healthy growth of scurvy-grass.

The chicks are guarded continuously at the nest until they are three or four weeks old. After their first flight, they may return to the nest for a few days for last feeds by the parents. At the end of the breeding season, the assembled adults often take off for a mass silent flight as dawn breaks and the light improves. But very soon the nest ledges are deserted.

Kittiwakes take a variety of food, from fish by way of shrimps, marine snails and terrestrial invertebrates, to plants, grasses and seeds. But they winter far out at sea. As scavengers they will follow a trawler in the hope of offal and will congregate around whale blows to enjoy breathy globules of grease. On the whole they forage far out at sea.

Canadian breeders migrate south, wintering along coasts and harbours to New York State. West Greenland birds remain there, while those from east Greenland go to join those in Iceland, whose population is resident. Some Svalbard birds may migrate to winter in northern Norway, many go to the Faroes and some reach the British Isles, to join the resident population there. Chukchi and Bering Sea birds winter south to the East China Sea and northwest Mexico.

KITTIWAKES AND VICTORIAN FASHION

In the latter part of the 19th century newly fledging kittiwakes were massacred mercilessly on the west country island of Lundy by British fishermen who collected the wings of juvenile birds and sent them to London for the fashion trade. This was at a time when it was regarded as the height of fashion to decorate hats with the plumage of dead birds.

'At Clovelly, opposite Lundy Island, there was a regular staff for preparing the plumes; and fishing smacks, with extra boats and crews, used to commence their work of destruction by daybreak on the 1st of August (when the close time under the Seabirds Preservation Act expired), continuing this proceeding for upwards of a fortnight. In many cases the wings were torn off the wounded birds before they were dead, the mangled victims being tossed back into the water... On one day 700 birds were sent back to Clovelly, on another 500, and so on; and, allowing for starved nestlings, it is well within the mark to say that at least 9000 of these inoffensive birds were destroyed during the fortnight.'

From Yarrell's *British Birds*, 4th edition, 1885

IVORY GULL
Pagophila eburnea

*Length
40–43cm
(17–18in)*

*Wingspan
108–120cm
(45–50in)*

Pure white, with a stout pale-yellow bill, a red eye-ring and short black legs, the ivory gull is somewhat larger than the kittiwake. A truly Arctic species, spending its whole life breeding and wintering entirely in the high Arctic above 70°N or, more precisely, above the July isotherm of 5°C. One of the very few birds (including the ptarmigan and snowy owl) which reacted to the last ice age by adapting to the severe cold and winter darkness and remaining year-round, when most birds migrate south for the harsh months. The webs between their toes are much reduced, by comparison with other gulls, to minimise heat loss. Their claws are curved to improve their grip on the ice, for the ivory gull is closely associated with ice in all its forms.

Although they catch fish and take crustaceans, ivory gulls are principally scavengers. There may be concentrations of ivory gulls along the ice edge of the

Davis Strait, especially near the pupping grounds of the hooded seal, where they find sustenance in afterbirths and dead pups. They are heavily dependent on the pickings from polar bear kills, tending to keep company with the bears in order to benefit from the remains of flesh and blubber which litter the killing ground. They follow dog teams and can be found around human habitation in the hope of handouts. In west Spitsbergen I have seen them land on ships for the same reason though the easiest place to see them is by the dog cage in Ny Ålesund.

Ivory gulls breed on Ellesmere, Devon and Baffin Islands in Nunavut, a few in Greenland. They are fairly well established in east Svalbard, while the main breeding area is in Franz Josef Land, Kong Karls Land and Novaya Zemlya.

They arrive at the breeding sites in June, singly or in colonies, which range from a few pairs to a few hundred. The colony is sometimes on level ground if it is free of predators, often on nunataks, sometimes high up on cliff slopes on the coast or some way inland. Unlike the sites of guillemot and kittiwake colonies, the locations are not too predictable – a well-known breeding place may unaccountably be abandoned. Although ivory gulls are markedly tolerant of human presence, seeming tame and fearless, disturbance by aircraft has caused wholesale abandoment of a colony.

The nest is a large pile of seaweed or moss. Two eggs, usually, are laid in late June or early July, incubated by both sexes for 24–5 days. In a level-ground situation, they run the risk of being taken by polar bears. The parents care for the chicks till fledging, which occurs at about 35 days. They winter along the edge of the pack-ice.

'The snow-bird, though so delicate in its appearance, is almost as ravenous as the fulmar, and as little nice in its food. It rarely alights in the water, but often sits on the ice, preferring the most elevated situations. Its voice is a loud and disagreeable scream.'
William Scoresby, An account of the Arctic Regions, Constable, 1820

The webs between the toes of the ivory gull are smaller than those of other gulls, to minimise heat loss. Their curved claws improve their grip on the ice.

ARCTIC TERN

Sterna paradisaea

*Length
33–35cm
(14–15in)*

*Wingspan
75–85cm
(31–35in)*

The only tern in the high Arctic. Circumpolar in distribution, breeding north to about 83°N. Well established in Alaska and Canada, coastal Greenland, Jan Mayen, Svalbard, Bear Island and along the Russian coast; it is rarer in Franz Josef Land. Further south it is well established, alongside the common tern, in Iceland, the British Isles and Norway.

In breeding plumage it has a dark crown, while the rest of the plumage is a light grey, with longer tail streamers than the common tern. The legs, feet and bill are a dashing scarlet. It hovers to plunge-dive to a shallow depth for small fish, like sandeels, and crustaceans, after a water's-edge search. Will hover and pick insects off the tundra exactly as it hovers and snatches small fish from the sea.

Birds may arrive at the breeding area in May before the snow has melted, gathering in colonies which can involve hundreds of noisy and aggressive pairs preparing to nest in the open, on low grassy islands, tundra flats or shingle bars. In June they dig a shallow scrape, mostly unlined, to furnish with between one and three eggs, incubated by both sexes for 20–4 days. The chicks leave the nest a couple of days after hatching. Many eggs and chicks are lost to Arctic foxes and skuas, and doubtless some to the Inuit and remote islanders – they are said to be supremely tasty! Fledging takes about three weeks, when they leave the nest area to go fishing along the edge of the tide.

If you are foolish or cruel enough to walk into an Arctic ternery, prepare to be attacked mercilessly. They will not hesitate to mount a spirited attack, diving fearlessly and screaming as they come close, drawing blood from an unprotected scalp. The prudent tern-watcher, even if standing at a reasonable distance, should carry a lofted stick, held high, for the tern will always attack the highest point of an intruder. It is best to leave them in peace, after admiring their mastery of aerobatics.

Towards the end of August Arctic terns leave for the long-haul flight to the other end of the planet, wintering in Antarctica, many of them in the Weddell Sea, around the pack – the greatest migratory movements of any bird. They enjoy a life of perpetual summer, travelling nearly 50,000 miles (90,000km) every year, in a life which may last 30 years.

At the northern end of its range, the Aleutian tern breeds in the region of the Bering Sea.

AUKS

Auks are black-and-white sea-going birds which come ashore only to breed on cliffs and cliff-slopes. At their breeding places they congregate in noisy clusters, standing upright in penguin fashion. Hunting prey they use their wings to 'fly' underwater in hot pursuit of small fish and plankton. Their wings are short and paddle-like, and their flight in air – though they are somewhat reluctant to fly at all – is fast, furious and direct.

GREAT AUK
Pinguinus impennis

Woodcut by Thomas Bewick, from his 'History of British Birds', Longman, 1847

Height 55–60cm approx (21.7–23.6in)

Wingspan 50cm approx (19.7in)

Sadly, extinct. The great auk was a giant razorbill, the largest of the auk family, which bred in Greenland and Spitsbergen at the northern end of its range. Not truly Arctic, at best a sub-Arctic species, it was once abundant, breeding in earlier times in large numbers in Newfoundland, Iceland and even south as far as the Mediterranean. They probably bred in gregarious communities, almost shoulder-to-shoulder like guillemots. It seems likely that first-year birds dispersing from the Newfoundland stock migrated north by way of the Greenland current to become established in Greenland. Others found their way to Svalbard, with the North Atlantic Drift.

Like the penguins of the southern hemisphere, to which they were not related, great auks travelled the evolutionary route to flightlessness. As superb divers, they found fish prey without difficulty – their wings were reduced to paddles because they had no need to fly. But flightlessness became their undoing: explorers and fishermen found them a convenient source of food, since they were so easy to catch. They were over-exploited for meat, eggs and feathers, and for bait. Large, unable to escape capture, tasty and present in significant numbers on easily accessible low islands, they were taken in ever-increasing quantities by the

European sealers and fishermen working the Newfoundland cod-banks from the 16th century. It is said that British and French fishermen herded them onto their boats for slaughter. They were probably already in decline by 1700, by which time they were confined to a handful of colonies in northern Canada. They inevitably suffered the downward trend so typical of over-exploited wild stocks. As they became uneconomical from the fishermen's point of view they became more valuable as glass-case specimens for the casual collector and as museum specimens. Ironically, the great auk's very rarity caused it to be hunted with ever greater zeal for 'academic' collections. The market value increased and the remaining breeding sites in Iceland were systematically raided in the 1730s and 1740s. On Funk Island, Newfoundland, the last individual was collected in approximately 1800; the last survivor on St Kilda was sighted in 1843. The last of all was taken on Eldey Island, off the south coast of Iceland, in 1844, to join the dodo as a pathetic memory.

Museum specimens are to be seen in the University Zoological Museum in Cambridge, and in various other museums, though many of them are mock-ups.

In Willughby's 'Ornithology', published in 1687, the extinct bird we now know as the great auk was captioned 'penguin'.

'PENGUINS' OF THE NORTH

The original English name for the great auk was 'penguin' (from the Latin 'pinguis' – fat). British and Portuguese fishermen carried the penguin name to the Newfoundland banks, the birds' stronghold. (There are several Penguin islands off Newfoundland still today.) It is a reasonable assumption that the southern hemisphere penguins got their name by way of the earliest Portuguese seamen when they explored southern Africa and South America. They transferred their version 'pinguim' of the only flightless bird they knew to this newly discovered family of flightless birds with an upright posture like the familiar bird of the north. The northern hemisphere auk family, whose members, quite apart from the extinct great auk, seem today to be on the evolutionary road to flightlessness, is not related to the penguin. The similarity between them is a classic example of convergent evolution, in which animals which live the same lifestyle tend to look like each other even though they are not related.

LITTLE AUK
(Dovekie)
Alle alle

Length
17–19cm
(7–8in)

Wingspan
40–48cm
(17–20in)

The most abundant of Arctic auks, the little auk has strongholds in Greenland – well over a million breeding pairs – and Svalbard – well over ten million breeding pairs – and has extended its range even to the northernmost part of Franz Josef Land. It is in competition with Wilson's storm-petrel for being the world's most numerous seabird. About the size of a starling, even smaller than a puffin, it has a tiny bill and a little, bull-like head on a compact body, with short tail and wings.

Little auks are highly gregarious birds, gathering at sea in great rafts inshore, taking off for mass aerobatics, almost darkening the sky, before coming ashore to their nests. Colonies are established near to areas of high plankton production, not far from the edge of the summer pack-ice and almost always in places where there is open water, at least when the young are due to hatch. Large colonies are established usually on an open sea-face, in frost-shattered scree slopes or eroded fissured cliffs, from sea level up to a few hundred metres. They prefer a gentle slope, offering easy take-off from their vantage points in rocks above the nest holes. The insubstantial nest, made of small stones with a bit of lichen or grass, is well hidden in a crevice or under a boulder. The single egg is laid in late June or July, incubation is by both sexes for something over 24 days, after which the chick is close-brooded for a few days before being fed by both parents. On emerging from the safety of the nest many chicks are taken by glaucous gulls or foxes. Parents and surviving young leave together for the sea when the adults endure a flightless period while they moult.

There is a great deal of chatter and gossip at breeding time, when off-duty birds spend a lot of time resting and preening on their vantage points. Disturbed by an intruder or a passing piratical gull, they erupt as a dense flock in a 'dread', sweeping over the hillsides with a curious laughing cry in a manoeuvre which presumably serves to confuse the predator. The resulting showers of faeces fertilise a luxurious growth of lichens and mosses. It is said that a Svalbard colony of 70,000 pairs benefits the land beneath it with 60 tonnes of faeces per square kilometre during the breeding season. The area below the colony is always marked by a lush growth of greenery nourished by these droppings. Mosses, lichens, scurvy grass and chickweed grow in abundance, in turn attracting herbivorous birds like ptarmigan. Early Dutch whalers collected the scurvy grass for their health and ate the leaves, raw or boiled.

The breeding season is timed to coincide with the seasonal peak of plankton and small fish. They specialise in taking copepods, amphipods and other small items from the plentiful zooplankton of midsummer. The total plankton harvest for a typical colony of 100,000 breeding pairs may amount to over 70 tonnes. Mostly the birds fish within a couple of kilometres of the colony, but often as much as 100km

'When on the ice, they generally sit in an erect posture. They dive quickly on being alarmed, and pass through the water, by the use of their wings, with great velocity'.
William Scoresby,
An account of the Arctic Regions,
Constable, 1820

out to sea. They fish at night, when their prey migrates to the surface, and carry their catch back to the chick in a throat pouch.

The Inuit of northwest Greenland are highly dependent on little auks for food in summer, when their coast is ice-free and they are unable to hunt for seals and whales. The birds are captured in flight by sweeping a 'flegg-net' attached to the end of a long pole. They are eaten raw or boiled; baked birds are eaten whole. It is also said that Inuits enjoy them raw after the birds have spent a couple of months fermenting in a blubbery sealskin sack. The Inuit also wove shirts from little auk skins, in the days before cotton underwear arrived on the scene.

In autumn little auks migrate: the Svalbard population moves south to the Norwegian Sea or across to southwest Greenland to survive by virtue of the great polynyas of the Davis Strait. Some go as far south as the British Isles, and individuals may reach the coast of Iberia. Occasionally little auks are driven ashore by storms and become 'wrecked', sometimes in large numbers, when settlements far from the sea become invaded by the bizarre sight of these tiny birds walking the streets, dazed by the lights.

Little auks take copepods when they come to the surface at night, stowing large numbers in their throat pouch, in order to carry them back, hamster-style, to the waiting chick.

COMMON GUILLEMOT
(Common murre)
Uria aalge

The main populations of this species occur south of the high Arctic, well away from the ice, but some hundreds breed on Jan Mayen, probably around a hundred on Spitsbergen, a healthy population in the order of a million on Bear Island and more millions in the Bering Sea.

The bill is slender and pointed, gannet-like for grasping a single fish longer than its bill. 'Bridled' individuals have a white, orbital eye-ring with a white line extending back. They find their food in dives which may last over a minute and reach down as deep as 60m. They swallow their catch before surfacing, unless they are taking it back to their chick. Sometimes a group of birds will join together in a line to circle and herd a shoal before picking off the fish at the edge.

Guillemots breed on ledges on vertical or near-vertical cliffs on the rocky coasts of offshore islands and stacks, densely packed in a 'seabird city'. Guarding the smallest breeding territory of any bird, they stand close together, often literally shoulder to shoulder with their neighbour, on noisy and crowded open ledges. On stacks, they will crowd together on the flat top in such numbers that there is a virtual carpet of birds.

They make no attempt at building a nest; the single, pear-shaped egg is laid on bare rock. Incubation takes 28–36 days, and the newly hatched chick is fed by both parents, with single fish carried back to the ledge head-first in the bill, pointing forward. The chicks huddle together on their precarious ledge, never walking more than a few token inches.

*Length
38–45cm
(15–18in)*

*Wingspan
64–73cm
(25–28in)*

A general raucous growling is characteristic of a guillemot colony, interspersed with the wistful and plaintive calls of the chicks.

Brünnich's Guillemot
(Thick-billed murre)
Uria lomvia

Length
39–43cm
(16–18in)

Wingspan
65–73cm
(27–30in)

Brünnich's is the most northerly of the guillemots. Breeding takes place from the Yukon coast, by way of Greenland, Bear Island (though this is the latitude at which the more southerly common guillemot *U. aalge* is more dominant), Svalbard, Franz Josef Land, Novaya Zemlya and the Siberian Arctic. It is hugely represented in the Bering Sea. This species has a curious white stripe on its bill – on the cutting edge of the mandible. Ashore or on an ice-floe, they stand upright in penguin style, like all auks. While, like most of the auks, Brünnich's guillemot is not an enthusiastic flyer, it is an expert diver and underwater swimmer. Its diet is almost exclusively small fish, like capelin, sandlance and the juvenile form of Arctic cod, but also squid, taken in dives which may reach a depth of 200m.

There are relatively few colonies, but those there are contain staggering numbers, sometimes well over a million birds. These large congregations serve to stimulate breeding activity, but may also help in disseminating useful information, such as the direction from which the most successful fish-carrying birds are coming.

The guillemot cities are sited on exposed cliffs, where the birds occupy ledges against the rock wall, protected from the depradations of Arctic foxes by sheer inaccessibility. One of the most impressive of these breeding sites is on the dolomite cliffs of Cape Fanshaw in the Hinlopen Strait between Spitsbergen and Nordauslandet, where the guillemots crowd together in clamorous strings on ledges which form a ladder from just above the water's edge to a hundred metres above the sea, in a seemingly vertical reach up to a series of medieval-looking castles, spires and towers.

The nest-ledges are occupied in March and April; a single egg is laid on the bare ledge after the snow melts in May or June. The incubation period is 31–4 days, with the parents taking turns in brooding. The chick is fed at the nest ledge for some three weeks – the parents travel many miles to collect fish. Fledging takes the best part of six weeks, but, amazingly, the chick leaves the nest ledge when it is only half-fledged, two or three weeks after hatching, at a time when it is totally unable to fly. Accompanied by its father, it launches itself over the edge, half-flying and half-fluttering, in a perilous fall to the sea below. Once safely afloat, the two of them begin the long migration journey. At this time the male parent is also flightless: he moults while he escorts the growing chick as they swim south. They overwinter in open water, south of the ice. Svalbard birds stay in the Barents Sea, while birds from west Greenland swim the Labrador current to winter on the Newfoundland Grand Banks, where fish are abundant.

Morten Thrane Brünnich was a Danish scientist of whom Linnaeus wrote, '…would that we had more Brünnichs; natural history would then be perfect.'

PURPOSE-DESIGNED EGGS

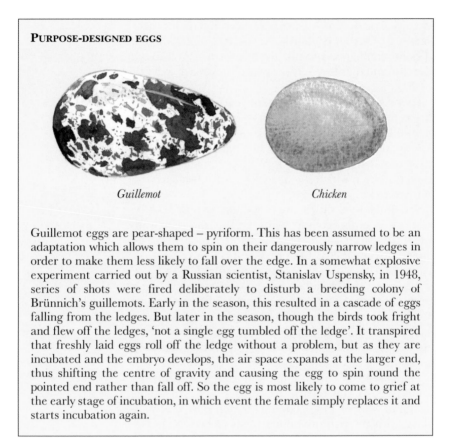

Guillemot   *Chicken*

Guillemot eggs are pear-shaped – pyriform. This has been assumed to be an adaptation which allows them to spin on their dangerously narrow ledges in order to make them less likely to fall over the edge. In a somewhat explosive experiment carried out by a Russian scientist, Stanislav Uspensky, in 1948, series of shots were fired deliberately to disturb a breeding colony of Brünnich's guillemots. Early in the season, this resulted in a cascade of eggs falling from the ledges. But later in the season, though the birds took fright and flew off the ledges, 'not a single egg tumbled off the ledge'. It transpired that freshly laid eggs roll off the ledge without a problem, but as they are incubated and the embryo develops, the air space expands at the larger end, thus shifting the centre of gravity and causing the egg to spin round the pointed end rather than fall off. So the egg is most likely to come to grief at the early stage of incubation, in which event the female simply replaces it and starts incubation again.

Brünnich's guillemots were taken in enormous numbers for food by the Greenlanders, perhaps half a million birds a year. The eggs, which are larger than a hen's egg, were much prized. It is said that as many as 10,000 a year are taken in the Upernavik district. At one time there was even a market for canned guillemot. In Novaya Zemlya they were salted for the market. After gross over-exploitation they are mostly now protected, at least on paper, but in recent years the population has suffered a serious decline, near terminal in the case of the Greenland population.

BLACK GUILLEMOT

(Tystie, sea pigeon)
Cepphus grylle

With its conspicuous white wing patches, this bird is unmistakable. Not as common as Brünnich's guillemot or the little auk, the black guillemot is nevertheless circumpolar in distribution, breeding in Arctic North America (where it is known as the sea pigeon from its habit of laying two eggs), Greenland, Iceland, Jan Mayen, Bear Island, Svalbard and points east to Siberia.

Less sociable than the other auks, it often hunts alone, but may join with others to form line-abreast on the water and herd fish. Strings of black guillemots are not an uncommon sight. They are strong swimmers, with a preference for shallow water, diving in the top

Length
30–32cm
(13–14in)

Wingspan
52–58cm
(22–24in)

five fathoms to search the bottom for fish, such as butterfish, and especially crustaceans and molluscs. They often fish close to the ice edge and by glacier snouts. On average they will be on the surface for 15 seconds before diving for as much as a minute, during which time they may have travelled as much as 75m. In the Arctic, crustaceans and molluscs are an important component of the diet.

They arrive at the breeding grounds to nest in May or June. Less gregarious than other auks, they may be found in a loose colony of a few birds or a few dozen. Easy-going in choice of nest-sites, they lay their eggs directly on to a shallow depression in a hole or crevice in scree or under stone slabs or boulders or driftwood behind the beach. Both sexes alternate shifts in incubating the two eggs for 23–8 days, then care for the chicks until they fledge at about 34–6 days. The chicks are independent soon afterwards.

Somewhat sedentary by nature, they do not go far in the winter, remaining in the north as long as there is open water for fishing. They feed in polynyas or at the edge of the pack-ice, even scrabbling to explore inside fissures.

Black guillemot numbers are healthy. Of a possible global population of some 300,000, large numbers are in the north, perhaps 100,000 in Nunavut and Baffin Bay, 50,000 in Iceland. But their tendency towards dispersed breeding has made it difficult to estimate numbers with any precision.

WHY 'GUILLEMOT'?

The derivation of 'guillemot' is controversial. It comes from the French, without much doubt. It is said to be a pet form of the Christian name Guillaume – William. An early English name for the common guillemot was Willock, or Willick or Willy. But another possibility is that it comes from *goéland* with the addition of *moette*. *Moette* is from the old German, found today as *möwe* – gull. 'Mew' is of course an old English word for gull. Guillemot may translate as 'wailing mewer'.

ATLANTIC PUFFIN
(Sea parrot, sea clown)
Fratercula arctica

U nmistakable at close range, the puffin is not so easy to identify in poor light and at a distance when it is easily mistaken for the other auks. This species is confined to the North Atlantic, but other puffins are found in the North Pacific. It is common nowhere in the high Arctic, which is at the edge of its breeding range and may hold something more than 10,000 birds. Populations include Greenland (a few thousand, mainly on the west coast), Jan Mayen (a foothold), Svalbard (possibly 10,000 pairs, increasingly evident around the coast of Spitsbergen) and Bear Island (some hundreds). In lower latitudes the puffin's world stronghold is Iceland. It is also established on the Lofoten and Faroe Islands and most easily seen on the seabird islands of northern Britain. Puffins also breed in Newfoundland in good numbers, and breed less well south to the coast of Maine.

Length
26–29cm
(11–12in)

Wingspan
47–53cm
(20–22in)

Puffins have long been regarded as choice items for the galley and the kitchen. In Iceland, to this day, there is an annual catch of the best part of 200,000. Nowadays it is mainly the full-grown newly aerial birds, which are taken in August by the skilful deployment of long-handled 'flegg-nets'. They are eaten boiled, stuffed, roasted, dried, smoked or salted.

Puffins are gregarious birds, nesting in sociable colonies on slopes. The nests are underground, in lower latitudes often in rabbit or shearwater burrows, but in the high Arctic, where there is less soil, they modify their requirements to choose crevices or the space under convenient boulders, rather in the style of razorbills.

'The puffyn hatcheth in holes in the cliffe, whose young ones are thence ferreted out, being exceeding fat, kept salted, and reputed for fish as coming nearest thereto in their taste.'
Richard Carew, 'Survey of Cornwall', 1602

The single white egg is incubated for 40–3 days. The chick is fed on a diet of small fish of sandeel size, though in the north chicks are probably also fed marine organisms, such as crustaceans and worms, when they are available. The adults are deep divers, reaching down as far as 70m to collect a beakful of fish, arranged neatly athwartships and held firmly in place by the corrugations of the mandibles. The chick stays in its safe underground retreat until it becomes even fatter than its parents, for a fledging period of 47–51 days, but towards the end of that period it is abandoned. After abandonment, it fasts for a week or so before emerging at night to find its own independent way to sea.

The horned and tufted puffins of the Pacific just reach into the Arctic in the Chukchi Sea around the Chukotka Peninsula. (See page 146.)

After the breeding season, part of the bill-covering is shed by the adults, producing a much more conventional shape and discarding the 'clown' image. They migrate south to winter far out at sea.

'Puffin' was originally the name given to the cured carcass of the fat manx shearwater fledgling, which was taken in large numbers for market. From medieval times until the end of the 18th century it was an esteemed delicacy in Britain. The young shearwater was corpulent – or puffed up – and the derivation 'puffling', now 'puffin', seemed a natural enough name for the salted bird.

It is not as clear how the word came to be applied to the sea parrot, as our *Fratercula arctica* (little brother of the Arctic) was known till well into the 19th century. Maybe it found its way back from the English markets to the Celtic seabird islands of Wales to be confused with the sea parrot which, like the shearwater, also nested in burrows. The scientific name of the shearwater is still *Puffinus*.

SNOWY OWL
Bubo scandiaca

A wholly Arctic bird, widespread in the tundra, the snowy owl is large and striking, yet, in spite of its conspicuous whiteness, it is a somewhat elusive bird. However, with luck, it may be seen perched in virgin whiteness on a convenient eminence. It may even astonish a seawatcher by flying past a ship at sea, on passage from lemming island to lemming island.

Length
53–66cm
(22–28in)

Wingspan
142–166cm
(59–69in)

Pure white, with a certain amount of black barring, it is well camouflaged against the snow. Well adapted to extreme cold, it has feathered trousers and its feet have pads which are covered by specialised corny feathers, which minimise heat loss and lift the bird off the icy ground.

Breeding success is heavily dependent on the availability of its principal prey, lemmings. In a good lemming year, the snowy owl has been seen as far north as Ellesmere Island, 82°N, in the Canadian Arctic. But it is seen only rarely as a vagrant on Svalbard, where rodents, like lemmings, are not present.

Snowy owls nest solo, though on the Canadian tundra they may be a magnet for the geese which form a colony around it to benefit by protection from Arctic foxes. The nest is built on the open tundra, a scratch on the ground making a slight depression on a knoll or slight rise which gives an extensive view. The number of eggs laid, and their timing, depends on the prospects for the lemming harvest (presumably the owl can hear lemming activity under the snow and assess abundance). Incubation begins with the first egg, so that there is always a dominant chick: if prey is hard to come by, he/she is the one to benefit while its siblings go under. The owl hunts over marshy tundra, silently and with moth-like flight – a stealth fighter. Lemmings are almost the only prey, although rarely they take small birds like snow or Lapland buntings. The young owlets enjoy two lemmings a day in a good year. Adults need between 600 and 1,600 full-grown lemmings in a year to sustain them.

Owl success depends on a healthy population of lemmings.

The owls remain in the Arctic for the winter, unless it has been a poor lemming year in which case they migrate south, usually without much long-term breeding success.

In the bad old days the Hudson Bay Company used to offer a quart of brandy for every owl killed, the justification for this unusual bounty being that they annoyed sportsmen by carrying off shot birds before they could be retrieved. The Inuit made fancy bags from owl skins.

LAPLAND BUNTING
(Lapland longspur)
Calcarius lapponicus

Like the snow bunting, the Lapland bunting is a truly Arctic bird, breeding from Alaska, northern Canada, Greenland, Svalbard and points east, though rarely in Severnaya Zemlya.

It is a bird of the open tundra and moss-heath, though in northern Scandinavia it frequents high mountains. Strikingly marked in summer plumage, it tends to perch conspicuously on top of a rock, or, in settlements, on rooftops, where it may sing like a skylark in defence of its territorial patch. On the ground, it runs about vigorously in search mainly of seeds. It may also forage along the tideline of the seashore.

The Lapland bunting may join with others in forming a small breeding colony. The young are raised on the insects which are abundant in the short Arctic summer. After the breeding season they migrate south, but their destinations are not yet fully understood.

Length
15–16cm
(5.9–6.3in)

Wingspan
25.5–28cm
(10–11in)

Adult female
Lapland bunting

SNOW BUNTING
(Arctic sparrow, snowbird)
Plectrophenax nivalis

Length
16–17cm
(6–7in)

Wingspan
32–38cm
(13–15in)

Also known as the 'Arctic sparrow', this is the most abundant songbird in high latitudes, indeed the only breeding passerine in Svalbard. Particularly common around settlements, it breeds mainly in the Arctic, where it enjoys a circumpolar distribution. There are isolated populations high up on mountains south of the Arctic. It is well established in central Asia.

Snow buntings are busy birds, hunting for insects and seeds over the tundra, boggy marsh, pools and sandy shores. (In lower latitudes they are birds of the high mountains.) Seeds are their main food.

Males are first to arrive at the breeding grounds, arriving in the late spring, when they take and hold individual territories. They sing their courtship song from the eminence of a boulder or hummock, sometimes from high in the sky like a skylark. When the females arrive, they pair and choose a hole. They then start building a secret nest of grasses, moss and lichens, lined with hair and feathers, while the male guards the property. Four to six eggs are laid, incubated for 12–14 days. The young are cared for by both parents, before they fledge and fly at ten to 12 days.

In the summer of 1896, while the great explorer Fridtjof Nansen was drifting with his ship *Fram*, deliberately stuck in the ice 200 nautical miles from Spitsbergen, a pair of snow buntings adopted the vessel, feeding on galley waste, carrying nest material and going through the motions of nesting.

Snow buntings breeding in Greenland migrate south to winter around the Great Lakes in central North America; those from Svalbard go to coastal northwest Europe. A few breed in Scotland, where they are joined by small numbers of wintering birds.

Female

'When we sailed near the ice, they came in great flocks to us in our ship, near the island of John Mayen, and were so tame that you could pick them up in your hands. They run upon the ice, where I only saw them, and not upon the land, which is the reason they are called snow-birds. They kept with our ship till we catche'd the first whale, and after this the other birds frightened them away. I can tell nothing of its singing, only that it whistelleth a little, as birds use to do when they are hungry.'

From the account of Friederich Martens
Voyage to Spitsbergen, 1671

Very few birds spend all year in the Arctic – perhaps only gyrfalcon, raven, ptarmigan, snowy owl, Arctic redpoll, Ross's and ivory gull; in polynyas, Brünnich's and black guillemots, and little auks.

NIGHT-TIME BEHAVIOUR
Even though daylight lasts the best part of 24 hours a day in the Arctic summer, the Arctic passerines tend to rest for a period of inactivity around midnight, much as birds of lower latitudes roost in the darkness of night. This quasi-roosting behaviour is less obvious among seabirds. Auks, for instance, feed actively at night, when fish and zooplankton tend to migrate to the surface.

TERRESTRIAL MAMMALS

Few mammals can endure the Arctic winter with its 24 hours of darkness, freezing cold and shortage of food. Those which survive are specially adapted to extreme climatic conditions, blessed with extra-thick pelage and well covered extremities. Small mammals like lemmings must avoid the worst of the cold, burrowing down so that they are covered with a blanket of snow and enjoying a temperature significantly warmer than at the surface.

Foxes, bears, reindeer and muskoxen build up a fat layer of blubber which may be several inches thick in the days of summer plenty, then grow thick winter coats to protect themselves from the icy wind. Reindeer hair is hollow, trapping a reservoir of warmed air. Winter coats are thicker and longer.

Given that animals are well insulated against the cold, their main winter problem is finding enough to eat. None of them hibernate; they are active throughout the year. Lemmings and reindeer find scanty resources of vegetation. Foxes rely to a certain extent on food which they cached in the summer, but they also benefit from being able to follow polar bears on to the sea ice in order to scavenge the remains of a seal kill. One welcome advantage is that any left-over prey from the days of summer plenty will remain in good condition in the refrigerated days of winter. In times of hardship even herbivores may become carrion-eaters.

Arctic fox in white winter pelage

LEMMING
(Collared lemming, snow lemming)
Dicrostonyx groenlandicus

The lemming is a common animal in the far north of Canada, Greenland and the Taimyr Peninsula, but not present in Svalbard, which accounts for the fact that there are no raptors there. Hamster-like and the size of a small rat, it is a stout blunt-nosed animal with a short tail and small eyes. Its ears are tucked away in abundant fur. Well adapted to a hard life in low temperatures and deep snow, its claws are enlarged as burrowing tools.

The lemming's main food is grass and the leaves of Arctic willow. Its dense fur turns white in winter, at which time it does not hibernate but lives along the slopes of raised beaches in a grass nest, composed of a principal tunnel with a series of side tunnels leading to the foraging areas. Provided there is a metre or so of snow above it will keep warm – the nest temperature may be 22°C warmer than the surface.

In favourable conditions, lemmings produce a first litter in March, while they are still under the snow. With a gestation period of less than three weeks, subsequent litters of half a dozen young may appear monthly through the summer months till September.

For reasons which are not entirely clear, lemming populations exhibit a classic three- or four-year population cycle, reaching high densities in what is known as a 'lemming year', only to crash subsequently in a steep decline resulting from food shortage, disease and stress. This cycle directly affects the fortunes of predators – such as Arctic foxes – and raptors – such as snowy owls and sea eagles.

Various bird and mammal species rely on the summer flush of Arctic vegetation without damaging its long-term viability, but in a good 'lemming year' the super-abundance of the rodents may cause serious damage. Over a period of years, however, the lemming population and its vegetation support reach a tolerable harmony.

Length
12.5cm
(5in)

Weight
120g
(5oz)

Lemmings endure cyclic population explosions which force them to make unwelcome migrations in search of food. They do not leap over clifftops for fun!

ARCTIC FOX
Alopex lagopus

...in summer pelage

*Length
85cm
(35in)*

*Weight
2–5kg
(4–11lb)*

Circumpolar and restricted to the Arctic, these foxes are most abundant in the coastal regions, although they wander freely over the sea ice. Often the only indigenous land mammal present in a region, for instance on Svalbard. They are small, much smaller than the red fox of lower latitudes, with a length of 46–66cm, of which more than half is tail. The dog is heavier than the vixen, varying between 2.9–3.6kg.

The Arctic fox has a short, blunt head with small furry ears and thick insulating underfur, all in pursuit of effective heat retention; it may survive in temperatures as low as -70°C. 'Gloger's Rule' says that terrestrial vertebrates tend to be white if they live in the far north, an adaptation to living with snow, and the Arctic fox is a perfect example, along with the polar bear and the ptarmigan. But in summer they are dimorphic, appearing in two forms – greyish-brown or smoky-grey. The smoky form, known as the 'blue' fox, is less common in the Canadian Arctic, but represents about half the population in Greenland, Jan Mayen and Iceland.

Rather solitary creatures for much of the year, nevertheless they enjoy a strong pair bond, reuniting at the family den for the breeding season between February and May. The den will be in sandy soil or soft ground, perhaps burrowed into a creek or lake bank, the side of a pingo or a dune ridge. It will have a series of tunnel entrances, and is very often sited alongside a seabird colony, of little auks for example. The vixen may breed in her first year, but more normally in her third, dropping an average of seven pups, but as many as 20. They are born in the underground den in the late spring after a 51–7 days gestation period. By mid-summer they will be weaned, at a time when the abundance or otherwise of food will have a major impact on success. At this time the dog fox will bring food to the den for the pups to learn to tear apart. They are cared for through the summer until they disperse to forage and fend for themselves. The foxes may not breed at all in a year when food is scarce.

Given fast ice or convenient ice floes to aid its travel the fox, which is perfectly capable of swimming short distances, may cover great areas in search of food. Whereas mainland populations prey mainly on rodents such as voles and lemmings, on the high Arctic islands much of the fox's food comes from seabird colonies and tideline carrion. Coastal individuals are heavily dependent on fish, eggs and young seabirds and the scavenging potential offered by polar bear leftovers. In fact they are opportunists, eating anything they can get hold of. Along the coast of east Greenland, foxes will establish themselves close to the cliffs where barnacle geese are nesting, in order to snatch the goslings as they leap off the nest ledges and while they are negotiating the scree boulders on their way to the grazing grounds of the tundra. In this activity they are greatly helped by the way the adult geese honk a distinctive call at the crucial moment of the jump.

Rising temperatures are encouraging northward expansion of the temperate red fox; Arctic foxes are in decline.

One of the prime reasons Arctic seabirds and waterfowl choose to nest on precipitous cliffs is because of the depredations of foxes. Eiders, however, nest on the ground, and if a fox should discover an eider colony, it may effectively destroy it entirely, by taking and caching the eggs. There is an inbuilt danger for the fox, for in the event of a delay in the sea freezing at the end of a successful egg and chick season, it may be isolated on a small island without any means of support except for any food it has already cached.

BROWN BEAR
(Grizzly)
Ursus arctos

Length
1.7–2.8m (5.6–9.2ft)

Weight up to
680kg (1,500lb)

Grizzlies dig the coastal tundra for roots but also for the arctic ground squirrel Citellus parryi – sik-sik or suslik. A big squirrel, this is much enjoyed by the Inuit for meat and clothing.

Once much more widely distributed, the grizzly has now retreated to the relatively few remaining wildernesses, but there is a fair chance of seeing one on the coastal Arctic tundra. Though closely related to the polar bear, it is a land-based animal. In colour, it is a mix of chocolate-brown, tan and sandy-buff. Unlike the polar bear, it is decidedly territorial, and aggressive in defence of its resident females.

As a tundra-dweller, the brown bear's diet contains a high proportion of plant food, including berries and roots. But it will hunt whatever mammals present themselves, from caribou/reindeer to lemmings and voles. Although they have been known to kill a seal, they are more likely to scavenge the sea ice, taking advantage of the leftovers from a polar bear kill.

The Sami people of Siberia regard them as sacred, treating them as messengers from the gods, worthy of proper respect while still a welcome food source.

Like its marine cousin, the grizzly is dangerous, as it is more inclined to attack than retreat.

REINDEER
(Caribou)
Rangifer tarandus platyrhynchus

The most northerly of all deer, the reindeer's range is circumpolar on the tundra. Sub-species of the reindeer range from Arctic Canada – the Peary caribou – by way of introduced animals in southern Greenland to Svalbard, where the smaller version *R. t. platyrhynchus* is closely related to the Siberian and Canadian reindeer and is presumed to have arrived via the winter ice from Severnaya Zemlya and Franz Josef Land. They are not related to the domesticated reindeer of Scandinavia.

Reindeer are all small animals, but the buck of this Arctic sub-species reaches only to about a metre at the shoulder. They range widely over the tundra and islands, are slow-moving and are relatively easy to approach. The population in Svalbard was in danger of extinction from hunting until it was given legal protection by the Norwegians in 1925; it is now

Length
males 160cm
(67in)
females 150cm
(63in)

Weight
males
60kg in winter;
90kg in summer
(132lb in winter,
198lb in summer);
females
40kg in winter;
60kg in summer
(88lb in winter,
132lb in summer)

moderately abundant. They are the only deer in which both sexes wear antlers, those of the males being particularly impressive on such a small body. Those of the females are less generous, being little more than forked spikes. Adaptation for the Arctic includes a thick coat and a hairy muzzle. The ears and tail are short, reducing loss of body heat. They have broad and deeply cleft hooves which splay out for support on snow.

In winter reindeer forage for lichens, in summer they graze the abundant vegetation of sedges and grasses, perhaps taking a few birds and bird eggs, even lemmings if they are available. During the summer months they patronise the coast to feed almost continuously in order to build up a layer of fat which will see them through the hard times of winter.

The rut takes place in September or October, when a dominant male holds a herd against intruders until towards the end when he is exhausted and lesser males have their wicked way. Males shed their antlers after the rut and grow replacements in the following spring. Females keep them through the winter, shedding after giving birth to the single calf in May or June. Lactation lasts three months, during which time mortality of the calves is high on account of predation by bears and foxes. In Greenland, sea eagles probably concentrate more on afterbirths and the opportunities arising from sick or injured calves than healthy young.

The Arctic reindeer tend to be more gregarious than those of lower latitudes, and they make impressive long-distance seasonal migrations.

Reindeer have broad and deeply cleft hooves which splay out for support on snow.

MUSK OX
Ovibos moschatus

As a result of successful introductions, musk oxen may be seen from northern Siberia, Wrangel Island and along the Canadian Arctic archipelago to western Greenland.

Tough and heavily built, they are protected from winter cold down to -50°C by a dense undercoat of woolly fur, topped by outer guard hairs which provide a skirt reaching almost to the ground. The inner fleece is called *qiviut* by the Inuit. Finest of all wool, it can be knitted to make fabrics of exceptional warmth while remaining very light in weight. Musk oxen are well camouflaged, moving ponderously over the tundra against a rocky landscape. Related to sheep, their horns are impressive: a broad flat boss covers the forehead in buffalo style, and the horns sweep down, out and up to sharp tips.

In summer, the oxen feed enthusiastically on the vegetation of the coastal tundra, mainly on the twigs of dwarf willow, in order to build up a thick layer of fat. In winter, they survive by losing weight and economising on energy requirements.

In the rut of high summer, the bulls produce the musk which gives the species its name. This serves as a territorial marker and plays its part in royal battles.

The herd of a dozen or so is under the control of a dominant bull. Their only serious predator, apart from man, is the wolf. Under attack, the herd gathers in a tight circle, enclosing the calves and lowering their heads to offer a ring of sharp horns to the circling wolves: an effective defence strategy, except against guns. Musk oxen can be dangerous, charging furiously if disturbed.

Height
to 150cm (5ft)
at shoulder

Weight
to 300kg (660lb)

MARINE MAMMALS

Those mammals which depend on the ocean environment live in profoundly different conditions than the few land mammals which must endure fearsome winter temperatures. While lemmings, musk oxen and foxes must find ways of dealing with temperatures down to -50°C, seals and whales bask in water which can never dip below -2°C. They face one serious problem, however. Dependant on a supply of fresh air for breathing, they must have access to the open air. Open-water polynyas may provide the answer, and they are a mecca for many animals, but in ice-bound waters they must break through the ice to create breathing holes, or drown.

Seals have very little body hair and rely on their dense blubber layers for protection against the cold. Blood circulates through this layer in order to warm the outer layer of skin to protect it from the danger of freezing.

Of the various whales which may visit Arctic waters, the only year-round residents are the bowhead, the beluga and the narwhal. Others may be seen in the summer, but these are the truly Arctic species. Their most obvious adaptation to the ice-covered waters of winter is their total lack of a dorsal fin, which would be a great inconvenience in navigating under ice and in breaking open breathing holes.

Polar bears live in a world which straddles land and sea, yet are primarily marine creatures, living in a world of sea and ice, depending largely on seals for their prey. Their fur is well adapted for the cold air, with transparent hairs which allow light to reach the black and heat-absorbing skin. The hairs are also hollow, filled with still air. In the sea their thick blubber layer and dense pelage protect them from the water temperature which in any case is warmer than the air above. Even their great paws are protected by fur around the soles.

POLAR BEAR
Ursus maritimus

Circumpolar and a decidedly marine mammal, the polar bear's whole life is associated with the pack ice. Normally living within 200 miles of the shore, polar bears travel as far north as the pole. From east Greenland to Novaya Zemlya there may be 5,000 individuals, 2,000 of them in Svalbard waters. Satellite tracking has shown that polar bears range widely between southern Svalbard and Novaya Zemlya.

The polar bear is a huge animal, especially threatening when it stands up on its hind legs. Males may be 2.6m long and weigh over 400kg, females rather less. A curiously small triangular head sits on top of a long neck and a massive body encased in a

Length
2–3m
(6ft 6in–9ft 9in)

Weight
males 500kg
(1,100lb)
females 150–250kg
(330–550lb)

'The polar bear is a
noble-looking animal
and of enormous
strength, living
bravely and warm
amid eternal ice.
He is the unrivalled
master of existence of
this icebound
solitude.'
John Muir, 1881

thick layer of blubber. It has a roman nose, small eyes and short, round, furry ears. Its long legs are covered with dense fur and its large feet are covered with fine hair even to the toes; the soles are densely hairy. It has yellowish-white fur throughout the year in aid of cryptic colouration – camouflage. The long guard hairs form a watertight outer coat over a soft and fluffy undercoat which traps a layer of air against the skin; this allows it to swim well without getting wet to the skin. Once out of the water a quick shake leaves the outer coat almost dry. The guard hairs are air-filled and exceptionally strong. If you are lucky enough to find a tuft of white hairs on the shore, try pulling one apart. If it breaks it belongs to a reindeer!

'…as the master walked along the ship, he heard a beast snuffe with his nose, and looking overboard he saw a great beare hard by the ship, wherewith he

cryed out, a beare, a beare; and with that all our men came up from under hatches, and saw a great beare hard by our boat, seeking to get into it, but we giving a great shout, shee was afrayd and swam away, but presently came backe againe, and went behind a great peece of ice, whereunto we had made our shippe fast, and climbing upon it, and

Theodore de Bry

boldly came towards our shippe to climb up the bow, but we had placed the sail on deck as a screen and lay with foure peeces at the capstan and shotte her into the body, and with that, shee ranne away; but it snowed so fast that we could not see whither shee went, but we guest that she lay behind a high hummock of ice.'

Gerrit de Veer (9 August 1596) in *The three voyages of William Barents to the Arctic Regions*, Hakluyt Soc, 1876

The polar bear is buoyant in the water, with its head held high. It is a strong swimmer, with seemingly endless stamina. One individual was GPS-tracked swimming continuously for 232 hours, covering a distance of 687km in water varying from 2 to 6°C. The bear's main prey is seal, including bearded and harp, but especially ringed seals. It has a keen sense of smell and can detect seal pups even beneath the snow.

Polar bears are solitary by nature, living perhaps the loneliest life on the planet, but there may be a gathering of numbers to take advantage of an abundance of food. Of course there is also interaction at the time of breeding – the only time both sexes meet. They court in the spring, but after copulation in early summer the male takes no further part in the process. Implantation is delayed, and the female takes to a den excavated in the snow in late October. One, sometimes two, helplessly weak cubs are born in the den in late December. At this time they are blind and almost naked, but their diet of rich milk – 30% butterfat – means that by the time the mother breaks free in April, the cubs have increased from a birth weight of 680g (1½lb) to a healthy 11kg (25lb). At this time, conveniently, ringed seals have just given birth and are at their most abundant and their most vulnerable.

The mother will take care of the cub or cubs, teaching them their predatory trade for a good two years before she abandons them to make their own way over the ice and the polar seas. Starvation is the commonest cause of mortality in the first couple of years after they are abandoned. The females breed only once every two years.

Summer is the lean time for polar bears. Deprived of the fast-ice with its breeding population of seals, they come ashore to snooze the time away on tundra meadows, eating eider ducks and chicks, grazing the sparse vegetation and searching for ripe berries. At this time they are hungry and dangerous. They need to be taken seriously.

Polar bears have been much persecuted in the past, especially by the Norwegians with the devilish 'self-

Gjelder hele Svalbard

Polar bears are highly dangerous animals. An alarming number of people have been killed. In their territory you should be protected by competent guides with suitable scaring devices and powerful firearms. In Svalbard this is a requirement of law.

kill' device of a gun set within a cage, offering a choice morsel to the inquisitive bear. In taking the meat, it releases the trigger. From the 1950s, they faced safari hunters. Since 1973, they have enjoyed circumpolar protection, at least on paper, allowing only native hunters a quota. Now they face global warming.

POLAR BEAR CAPITAL OF THE WORLD

Go to the town of Churchill in Manitoba, Canada. You can't travel there by road (there isn't one), but you can visit by sea or train or plane. The human population of some 800 is outnumbered in October/November by a transient influx of perhaps a thousand bears. They are waiting for Hudson Bay to freeze. Hungry, after a summer existing on precious little but berries, they are anxious to shake the dust of Churchill off their paws. As a nuisance round town, they run the risk of being tranquilised and held temporarily in 'jail' waiting for the ice to release them.

Though not welcomed by the Churchill residents, who tend to discourage them with explosive fire crackers, they nevertheless represent lucrative tourist potential. Safely ensconced in a 4 x 4 tundra-buggy visitors will be driven out of the town and towards the coast where the bears are waiting for the sea ice to be strong enough to allow them back on the ice for the seal-stalking season.

As if the bears weren't enough of a reason to visit, there are also beluga whales in fair numbers. And if you wait till the New Year, Churchill offers a good view of the Northern Lights.

SEALS

Seals are well adapted to aquatic life in polar regions, cushioned and insulated from the cold air as effectively as they are from cold water with a thick coat of blubber and dense pelage. There are two main divisions – or Superfamilies – in the Pinnipeds. First the *Otariidae* which includes fur seals, sea lions and walruses. In the Arctic, the main representative of these 'eared' seals is the walrus (although the northern sea lion has a stronghold in the Bering Sea – see page 150). The other major grouping is the *Phocidae*, the 'true' seals which have no protruding external ear, cannot run or raise themselves on fore-flippers, cannot swivel their hind flippers and must clumsily haul or hump themselves on land in caterpillar fashion. These are well represented in the Arctic.

Fur seal skeleton

True seal skeleton

Seals have torpedo-shaped bodies superbly designed for fast underwater travel. Their nostrils are closed and sealed by muscular contraction as they enter the water and they exhale before diving to reduce the amount of air in their lungs, deriving the necessary oxygen from their well-supplied blood systems. Their heart-rate reduces and slows and their metabolism is reduced. On surfacing it is several minutes before their heart-rate returns to its usual surface beat.

Breeding must occur ashore, but they are comfortably able to pup on the fast ice. Males and pregnant females gather annually at the breeding place, where copulation takes place soon after the previous year's pups are fully grown. Implantation is delayed for three months so that although the gestation period is nine months the annual cycle is maintained.

Polar bears and killer whales are their natural enemies, but seals have also suffered greatly from the depredations of human sealers.

WALRUS

(Sea horse)

Odobenus rosmarus

*Length
males 250–340cm
(104–142in)
females 215–290cm
(86–121in)*

*Weight
males 750–1,400kg
(1,650–3,087lb);
females 500–900kg
(1,100–1,980lb)*

The Pacific walrus (Bering Sea and Russian far east) is the largest and most numerous of the walruses. The sub-specific Atlantic walrus is found in the northern part of the Davis Strait, the northern coasts of Greenland, Svalbard, Novaya Zemlya and the Laptev Sea. They inhabit shallow water off the Arctic coasts, usually close to land, tending to migrate south with the ice in autumn and north as it recedes in the spring. Creatures of the ice, they live on substantial floes in the moving pack, though they penetrate closer to the shore when the fjord ice breaks up in July. They may come ashore in places like Moffen Island, north of Spitsbergen, Franz Josef Land, Hudson Bay or the Chukorka peninsula and Wrangel Island. Sometimes they haul out ashore in astonishing numbers, maybe several thousands, when they tend to lie almost on top of each other, a classic example of thigmotaxis – 'bodies in close contact' – but they are highly vulnerable to human disturbance at this time. The largest concentration, of perhaps 20,000, is in the Bering/Chukchi Sea area. In the Canadian Arctic and west Greenland there are perhaps 25,000 individuals.

As with the seals, the powerful hind flippers supply propulsion while the fore-flippers are control surfaces, operating as rudders at slow speeds. The huge body is topped by a small head with small eyes. They have poor eyesight, but excellent hearing and sense of smell. The broad snout blossoms with hundreds of stiff moustache bristles. The most remarkable upper canine teeth project down and grow to as long as 100cm in the male, 60cm in the female. (Pacific males have longer teeth than those of the Atlantic.) The scientific name for walrus means 'toothwalker'. There has been much controversy in the past about the function of these remarkable tusks: they are certainly a useful tool when the animal is hauling itself up on to an ice-floe and in repose they lean on them.

The females are sexually mature at about five or six years of age, the males from about seven, though they are unlikely to get an opportunity to mate till several years later. Breeding activity is at its peak in April and May, with calves being born from April to June. Twins are rare, as with the seals. The single calf enjoys single-minded solicitude from its mother, who offers rich milk and suckles for as long as two years, maybe even longer if she is not pregnant with her next calf. Young breeding females may calve every two years but older ones have a more relaxed attitude and may breed every three or four years. The young animal has a dark skin which becomes paler with age till some old bulls seem almost albino.

Walruses are mainly bottom-feeders in shallow water, diving to take invertebrate food at depths up to 80m, though normally in dives of several minutes between 10m and 50m. The tusks may be used to work their way over the muddy/gravelly bottom, but it is the stiff facial whiskers which feel for the hidden molluscs

'The walruses here are very numerous, lying in herds upon the ice and plunging into the water to follow us as we passed. The sound they utter is something between bellowing and very loud snorting which, together with their tusks, make them appear as indeed they are, rather formidable enemies'.
Sir Edward Parry
HMS Hecla,
off Spitsbergen,
22 June 1827

In the high Arctic, walruses are much prized for their tough skin. It is used for covering kayak frames, and requires less sewing than seal skins because the hides are bigger. In places walrus skin is as much as 5cm thick, making it a first-class material for use as a rubbing-strake, protecting the vulnerable waterline from the graunching ice. It has even been used for drive-belts in industrial Europe. Mostly, however, walruses have been persecuted for the ivory of their tusks – an old male may have 5.35kg of ivory.

– a prime item of diet. The animal uses its powerful lips to suck out the muscle and the siphon parts of clams and mussels and spits out the shell. Other, less shelly, invertebrates and small fish are eaten whole, and it seems that walruses ingest a lot of gritty sand which is duly dispatched from each end.

In Svalbard they were nearly exterminated by hunters in the 19th century, then reduced to a pathetic remnant of their once flourishing status by the middle of the 20th century. The population has been protected since 1952, since when it has increased to a possible 2,000 individuals. It may be that the relative abundance on Franz Josef Land has aided the recolonisation; flipper-tagging has shown that migrant animals move across from east Greenland. Now there are fears that tourism pressures may affect this success as the walrus freely abandons traditional haul-out places in response to human disturbance. It is prudent to avoid getting too close to them, especially in a boat, since they are prone to attack or to attempt to climb in to join you.

Apart from some subsistence hunting by the Inuit and by some residents of Greenland, the walrus is now protected by law. But with elephant ivory politically unacceptable and only illegally marketed, it may be that the unfortunate walrus will again become the target of ivory-hunters, placing their slow recovery from decline in jeopardy. They need all the help they can get.

An early walrus hunt. Engraving from 'Historia de Gentibus Septentrional', 1555. Note that the tusks emerge from the wrong jaw!

RINGED SEAL
(Hair seal)
Phoca hispida

The ringed seal is a strictly Arctic species, seen in high latitudes to the pole itself, and widely distributed in the Canadian Arctic, Greenland, Svalbard, Novaya Zemlya and the Siberian coast. It is also found in the North Pacific, Lake Baikal and the Baltic and Caspian seas. The ringed seal is the smallest and most abundant of the Arctic seals: it reaches a maximum length of 150cm and weighs up to 100kg. It is shy of close approach, with good reason, since it is the favourite prey of polar bears. These seals are marked with grey-white rings on dark grey backs, while their underparts are generally an unspotted silver.

The females breed at four or five years old; the males are sexually mature at about five to seven years. The pregnant female prepares an underground lair on the fast ice or in snow. It is dug in a snowdrift or in the ice of a pressure ridge, out of sight of predators, though its main function seems to be to give the pup a relatively warm place in which to fatten, since Arctic foxes and

Length
120–150cm
(50–62.5in)

Weight
60–100kg
(132–220lb)

bears are perfectly capable of smelling them out. Wherever the lair, they maintain a breathing hole, scratching with sharp claws through as much as nearly 2m of solid ice. The pup is born in late April or May, with a white woolly coat. Unusually for seals, it is not weaned for as much as two months, by which time it has shed its natal coat for its first swimming suit of silver. By this time the lair has succumbed to the summer thaw and collapsed, so the young seal basks in the sun on the ice. In June and July the adults also moult, hauled out on the ice. While spending most time lying flat, they nevertheless keep a constant watch for polar bears, continually raising their heads to check for potential trouble.

Ringed seals feed on pelagic organisms and under-ice fauna, mainly crustaceans and polar cod. The average life span may reach 15 or 20 years, but they may live over 40 years.

Ringed seals are hunted by a variety of predators. Arctic foxes take some young pups. Killer whales, Greenland sharks and glaucous gulls are also predators, but the main predator is the polar bear. In Svalbard a few ringed seals are taken every year for dog-meat. Ringed seals are taken by commercial fur-hunters in the newly moulted stage, known in the trade as 'silver jars'. They have also been much exploited by the Inuit for food (flesh, liver and intestines), for lamp oil and for clothing and as kayak skins.

'The meat of these young animals is tender and free from oiliness but it certainly has a smell and a look which would not have been agreeable to any but very hungry people like ourselves. We also considered it a great prize on account of its blubber, which gave us fuel sufficient for cooking six hot messes for our whole party, though the animal only weighed thirty pounds in the whole.'

John Ross, on Parry's expedition,
from *A Voyage of Discovery*, 1835

BEARDED SEAL
Erignathus barbatus

A strictly Arctic species, the bearded seal is widely distributed and circumpolar, abundant in shallow waters around the coast, wherever there are leads and polynyas among the drift-ice. Svalbard individuals have been satellite-tracked on movements across to Jan Mayen and southeast Greenland.

The largest of the Arctic seals, their bodies are cigar-shaped, yet with a small head, decorated with a splendidly long and bushy moustache. Lacking the rings and spots of other northern seals, this species has a more-or-less uniform light to dark grey pelage. When wet, the pelage is dark and the moustache hairs droop, but as they dry in the sun the coat turns grey and the moustache perks up. They have strong claws on the fore-flippers, used in maintaining breathing holes, though they tend to patronise fairly thin ice, avoiding the serious fast-ice which is home to ringed

Length
200–250cm
(83–104in)

Weight
250–350kg
(550–770lb)

seals; they are more usually found associated with moving pack-ice.

On the whole they are solitary animals, not gathering in sociable herds, and typically they allow a surprisingly close approach. However, they tend to lie at the edge of a floe, within a short distance of the safety of water.

Bearded seals are sexually mature at five or six years in the case of the cows, six to seven years for the bulls. Pups are born on the ice from April to early May and are able to swim from birth. They are nursed for 12–18 days, by which time their weight has nearly trebled. They are then abandoned to moult before they begin active hunting.

The strikingly luxuriant moustache hairs are sensory organs of touch, used by the seal in exploring the sea-bed to locate crabs and shrimps in the benthos. They take clams and other molluscs and some bottom fish.

Their main predators are polar bears and man. The Inuit regard them as an important source of meat, lamp-oil (from the blubber) and clothing. Their bones become tools, their hides are used for the soles of shoes and for the outer skins of *umiaks* (kayaks). Chewed sealskin is used for *kamitt* – traditional waterproof shoes. (The word *mukluk* is also used in this context but has been hijacked by the fashion trade.)

Bearded seal. From Sir William Jardine, 'The Naturalist's Library', vol VIII, London, 1839

HARP SEAL
(Greenland seal)
Phoca groenlandica

An earlier scientific generic name for the harp seal was *Pagophilus*, or 'ice-lover', from the Greek, a wonderfully apt description for a seal which gathers in huge numbers on the ice in the far north. There are three discrete populations: one in the White Sea, one in the Greenland Sea south of Jan Mayen and one in the Davis Strait. The male grows up to 183cm in length and weighs up to 135kg. The female is smaller and lighter. The harp pattern is typical of older animals.

They are pelagic by nature, not seals of the inshore and coastal waters. In summer they are to be found in the very far north, rarely encountered around Svalbard, the most likely part being East Spitsbergen – Nordauslandet. In winter they migrate south, in spring they gather sociably in large numbers, following the retreating ice sometimes in herds of many hundreds, to pup and mate on the ice. Born on the ice, it must be a severe shock for the pup to emerge from the warm uterus to a fearsome cold world,

Length
150–200cm
(63–83in)

Weight
100–150kg
(220–330lb)

relieved only by suckling on rich warm milk which is almost the consistency of butter. The baby white coat, so valuable to commercial sealers, is moulted at two to four weeks to a spotted grey. As with other seals, the bulls are on hand to mate shortly after the pups are born. The two sexes only meet at this time, at 12-month intervals. Since the gestation period for harp seals is seven and a half months, after copulation the implantation of the blastocyst is delayed to adjust for the 12-month cycle – the pups are always born in the spring. Once weaned, at a month or so of age, the pup is abandoned by its mother to find its own way to the sea, feeding at the ice edge on crustaceans – shrimps, isopods and amphipods – and small fish. The pup migrates north as the ice retreats, to feed on the summer abundance.

After a number of changes of coat, harp seals finally adopt the 'harp' pattern when they reach sexual maturity: at about six years for the females, eight for the males. Adult harp seals are deep divers, staying underwater for many minutes at a time. They take a varied diet of pelagic fish such as polar cod, herrings and capelin, some benthic fish and crustaceans.

Harp seals have been hunted for subsistence and for the fur trade. Heavily exploited, the species has compensated by increasing growth rates. The harvest of 'whitecoat' pups in Canadian waters is controlled as a percentage of the herd size, estimated by aerial censusing.

Harp seal. From Sir William Jardine, 'The Naturalist's Library', vol VIII, London, 1839

HOODED SEAL
(Bladdernose seal)
Cystophora cristata

F̲ound in the Davis Strait, Greenland, Jan Mayen
and Svalbard, the hooded seal is a sea-going
animal of deep waters and is a deep diver. It is less
common than the harp seal and mainly solitary in its
early years. It is usually associated with drifting ice-
floes. The bull has an inflatable sac on its nose which
can be blown out to create the 'hood'. Its function is
presumed to be in courtship display and intimidation
of other males. The species varies widely in size, growing
up to between 133 and 245cm in length – the female
is smaller than the male. Her weight may reach 180kg.

Hooded seals pup on the ice south of Jan Mayen and
off Newfoundland in late March, in the middle of a
convenient ice floe; the newborn animal is attended by
its parent and by a group of hopeful males. The pup is
a particularly attractive baby, silvery-grey with a dark
face – known to sealers as a 'blueback'. It grows fast
and fat on a daily dose of highly concentrated milk

Length
males 250–300cm
(104–125in)
females 180–220cm
(75–92in)

Weight
males to 400kg
(1,180lb)
females to 180kg
(396lb)

which is more like the consistency of butter, something like 50% fat, and is weaned at two weeks, perhaps the shortest weaning period of any mammal. This is the moment the attendant males are waiting for – the cow is now in oestrus.

The newborn pup is a precocious swimmer and deep diver. A month-old hooded seal pup was recorded diving to 75m.

After the pupping and mating season the seals repair in June or July to traditional moulting areas on the icefloes in the Denmark Strait, south of Jan Mayen, and remain there until August, when they migrate south to the open sea between Svalbard and Bear Island. Their main food is probably various fish and squid.

Polar bears hunt pups in the spring but so do humans, the most serious predator. They have been hunted since at least the 18th century, first by whalers who used them to top up their whale catch, nowadays by sealers from Norway and Newfoundland who are looking for the 'blueback' pelts. The young pup wears a pelt which is prized in the fashion industry. Greenlanders take several thousand juveniles a year as a subsistence food but also for pelts.

'To the Esquimaux, the seal is of as much importance as bread is to a European. Its flesh forms their most usual food; the fat is partly dressed for eating, and partly consumed in their lamps; the liver when fried, is, even among sailors, esteemed as an agreeable dish. The skin, which the Esquimaux dress by processes perculiar to themselves, is made waterproof. With the hair off, it is used as coverings, instead of planks, for their boats, and as outer garments for themselves; shielded with which, they can invert themselves and canoes in the water, without getting their bodies wet. A single effort with their paddle restores them to their proper position. It serves also for coverings for their tents, and for various other purposes. The jackets and trowsers made of skin by the Esquimaux are in great request among the whale-fishers for preserving them from oil and wet.'

William Scoresby, *An Account of the Arctic Regions*, Constable, 1820

WHALES

Whales, dolphins and porpoises are members of the order Cetacea. They are totally adapted to a life at sea but, as air-breathing mammals, they must surface to breathe. Modifications to the standard mammal design involve a hairless fish-shape encased in a thick layer of insulating blubber, the nose on top of the head, forefeet becoming paddles, effective loss of hind feet and the tail becoming a horizontal fluke. Supported by water, they are free to grow to a great size and weight. They are divided into two broad suborders, the Odontoceti (toothed whales with a single blowhole) and the Mysticeti (whalebone or baleen whales with a double blowhole).

In diving, the blowholes are firmly closed and the heart-rate is slowed down. Whales are tolerant of a high concentration of carbon dioxide in the blood with which they are plentifully supplied; the result being that they are able to hold their breath for periods that would drown land animals. The breathing passages are separated from the gullet so that they are able to feed underwater without choking.

Working in murky water and at great depths, toothed whales find their prey by echo-location, using ultrasonic pulses which are inaudible to human ears. They also communicate within their group with trills, whistles, grunts and groans, which are perfectly audible above water.

Baleen whales have a profoundly different method of feeding. In relatively shallow water, they plough through the concentrations of plankton (possibly finding them by taste), gulping great quantities of water, expelling it through filter-plates of whalebone by contracting the ventral grooves of the throat and pressing the large tongue against the roof of the mouth, then swallowing the catch of uncountable numbers of small shrimps and larval fish. Not needing the agility and manoeuvrability of the hunting whales, they enjoy the advantages of greater size. The blue whale is the largest animal ever to live on earth – 30m long and weighing 150 tonnes.

'Leviathan...
Upon earth there is
not his like, who
is made without fear.
Will he speak soft
words unto thee?'
Job 41

Blue

Fin

Humpback

Minke

Killer

Pilot (long-finned)

The three truly Arctic whales, bowhead, narwhal and beluga, do not have dorsal fins, an adaptation that fits them for working under ice (and of course they are well supplied with heat-retaining blubber). But it is possible to see several other species of whale in Arctic waters, especially in the summer. Fin, humpback, minke and pilot whales have been recorded commonly, and even the blue whale is sometimes seen in the coastal waters of the Denmark Strait in summer. There is always the chance of killers.

GLOSSARY OF WHALE WORDS

Baleen Comb-like plates of bony material growing from the upper jaw of Mysticeti whales

Blow Moist air forcibly exhaled from the lungs through the nose (blowhole)

Breach To jump clear of the water's surface

Bubble-netting Behaviour associated with humpback whales, when they dive in a spiral, exhaling bubbles to enclose a shoal of pelagic fish which they then engulf from below, erupting explosively from the surface

Cetacean Member of the order Cetacea: whales, dolphins and porpoises

Dive pattern The typical sequence of dives and blows for a given whale species

Falcate Of the dorsal fin, meaning strongly curved or hooked

Fluke Propelling surface of a cetacean tail

Gam A sociable pod of gossiping whales, but also a social visit between whaling captains on a quiet day

Lobtail Slapping the surface with a tail

Lunge-feed Of baleen whales, describes lunging along the surface in pursuit of plankton

Melon Bulbous forehead of toothed whales

Pod Group of cetaceans travelling together

Rostrum Upper jaw

Sound Diving to depth, as when the humpback reveals its tail

Spyhop To poke the head vertically out of the sea

BLUE WHALE
(Sulphur-bottom)
Balaenoptera musculus

Length
to 30m (98ft)

Weight
to 150 tonnes

The largest animal which has ever lived on the planet is named for its bluish-grey skin seen at its best underwater. The Latin 'musculus' is variously taken to mean 'muscular', or as a diminutive of the latin 'mus', for 'mouse', which just may be an 18th-century Linnean joke.

The blue whale has a huge, mottled, metallic-blue-grey body, a flat head, and a small, hook-shaped dorsal fin placed well back towards the slender and graceful fluke. It is slow-moving, with a straight and powerful vertical blow – not bushy – which may reach nearly 10m, especially in cold air. It generally breathes in shallow dives at 20-second intervals before diving for half an hour. After the spout, the long expanse of back rolls over, with the small dorsal fin emerging just before the tail fluke makes a brief appearance. The speed of a blue whale is about 3 or 4 knots (6–8km/h).

Blue whales travel solo or in small groups, but may congregate at particularly rich feeding waters. In the Arctic summer they feed on krill, taking some

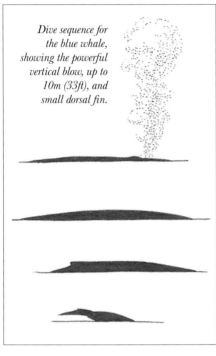

Dive sequence for the blue whale, showing the powerful vertical blow, up to 10m (33ft), and small dorsal fin.

8,000kg in a day, which may amount to a staggering eight million shrimps. When the pack-ice extends south at the onset of the Arctic winter, blue whales move south towards the warm tropical waters, where they live off their blubber reserves and gather in individual groups for courtship and mating (the male's penis is over 3m/9ft long) at about ten years of age. The gestation period is nearly 12 months, so the single calves are born in the warm waters in which they were conceived. They are nursed for more than six months, by which time they are over 15m in length and begin to take their share of the krill. They are sexually mature when they reach 23m in length. Females are thought to breed every three years. If the calf survives the first few years it may expect to live an average 35 to 40, though the exception may reach over 80.

Blue whales are widely distributed throughout the seven seas, both along shelf waters and the pack edge, and in open water. Their oceanic movements are little known. There are several discrete stocks, based in the North Pacific, the North Atlantic (where they are regularly seen in summer around a drop-off WSW of the Icelandic Snaefelisnes peninsula) and the southern hemisphere. Numbers were devastated by ill-regulated whaling in the 20th century, and progressively effective protection has so far failed to promote a real recovery. Their total world population may be in the region of 10,000. Their natural predators are gangs of killer whales which have been seen to attack, biting at their flukes and mouthparts.

FIN WHALE
(Finback, razorback)
Balaenoptera physalus

A regular summer visitor to the Arctic, the fin whale is similar in shape to the much rarer blue whale, but smaller and with a larger dorsal fin (the prominent dorsal gives the fin whale its common name). It is dark-grey to brownish-black on back and sides, the back being ridged from the dorsal fin to the flukes (the 'razorback'). Curiously, the head is dark on the port side and much paler on the starboard. Also on the starboard side the lower lip and baleen plates are yellowish-white while those on the port side are more blue-grey. These irregularities are presumably connected with the way in which the animal scoops its plankton catch when it rolls over on its side, so that

*Length
to 27m
(88ft)*

*Weight
to 90 tonnes*

Fin whale dive sequence showing the vertical blow, up to 6m (20ft). Tail flukes may not appear.

the starboard side becomes the under-surface and its mouth engulfs krill in a sideways fashion.

As the fin whale surfaces, the blow comes first – a tall spout spraying to 6m (20ft) and blossoming at its full height – followed by a slow roll and the appearance of the fin, but not the tail. Four or five blows occur at intervals of 10–20 seconds, the final roll before the dive revealing more of the back and possibly the tail. In a deep dive the animal may be down for nearly half an hour.

Fin whales occasionally leap clear of the water in a breach. Often solitary, they may also travel in pairs or in small social groups and not uncommonly will join a ship and travel in station off the beam. They are fast movers, able to cruise all day at a comfortable 7 knots but to sprint at 18 knots, a speed which saved them from the attention of the whalers until the arrival of fast catcher boats.

'Greatest of all is the Whale, of the beasts
  which live in the waters,
Monster indeed he appears, swimming on
  top of the waves,
Looking at him one thinks that there in the
  sea is a mountain,
Or that an island has formed, here in the
  midst of the sea.
He also sometimes his hunger (which worries
  him often most greatly),
Wishes at once to relieve, warm is his wide
  open mouth,
Whence he then sends forth breaths of odours
  as sweet as the flowers.'
Abbot Theobaldus of Monte Cassino,
A metrical bestiary, c1022–1035

HUMPBACK WHALE
Megaptera novaeangliae

A cosmopolitan species, the humpback whale is found in all the oceans and ranging from the tropics to the edge of the ice. In the North Atlantic, one group is found from east Greenland to the Barents Sea, while the other works from the south of Greenland to breed in the Caribbean.

The humpback is a stoutly robust whale whose colour ranges from all-black or grey to black upperparts and white below. The small dorsal fin sits on a raised hump (the humpback) with a series of smaller bumps leading to the tail. The most striking feature is the extraordinarily long flippers, nearly a third of the body length, some 5m (16ft) long. The flippers are white or nearly white and, together with

Length
males 15m
(49ft)
females 16m
(52ft)

Weight
to 48 tonnes

the tail flukes, are irregularly scalloped at the edges. The head, lower jaws and chin are covered with fleshy knobs – tuberosities.

Humpbacks cruise slowly, at 4–6 knots, but they are powerful enough to leap clear of the water frequently in spectacular breaching. Their dives are mostly for less than 15 minutes, maybe up to 20. They may occasionally 'lobtail', bringing the tail down explosively on to the surface, presumably as some form of warning. Their feeding technique is simply to engulf the krill swarms, either just under the surface or by lunging up to them from below.

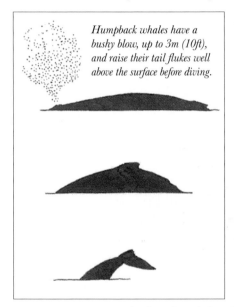

Humpback whales have a bushy blow, up to 3m (10ft), and raise their tail flukes well above the surface before diving.

Humpbacks travel mostly in small groups, but may congregate in herds of a dozen or so. They are coastal animals, moving along predictable migration routes. Given that they are also slow-moving, this made them easy prey in the old whaling days, with the result that their world stocks are now sadly depleted and slow in recovery. Apart from man, their main enemy is the killer whale. They are usually infested with whale lice and host large numbers of barnacles.

Humpbacks can be identified as individuals from the diagnostic markings on their tail flukes. If you have a fluke photo, please send a copy to: Rosemary Seton, North Atlantic Humpback Whale catalogue, Allied Whale Mammal Research Laboratory, College of the Atlantic, 105 Eden St, Bar Harbour, Maine 04609, USA

MINKE WHALE
(Piked whale, lesser rorqual)
Balaenoptera acutorostrata

The smallest and most abundant of the rorquals, with a streamlined but perhaps less slender body than its larger relatives, the minke whale has a narrow, pointed and triangular rostrum, with a ridge on top of a flat head. The upperparts are black; the underparts white from the chin back. There is pale grey blazing on the flanks, one above and behind the flippers and one in front of the fin. The tall, pointed dorsal fin is set well back on the body, and a pointed pectoral flipper sometimes has a strikingly white band across its middle in the northern population. They are often found close inshore.

Minkes are fast, dolphin-like swimmers, travelling on the surface at speeds up to 16 knots. They are fairly commonly attracted to vessels, keeping station or even diving from side to side.

Average length
males 8m (26ft)
females 9m (30ft)
max 10.7m (35ft)

Weight
5,800–7,250kg
(12,790–15,986lb)
maximum 9,000kg
(19,845lb)

Captain Minke was a Norwegian whaler who boasted of huge whales but actually captured small ones...

The blow is low and insubstantial, sometimes almost invisible; the animal often begins its blow before it has surfaced. Normally the breathing sequence involves five to eight blows at intervals of less than a minute, followed by a dive lasting perhaps 20 minutes. The fin surfaces with the blow. On diving, the tail stock is arched high, but the fluke does not appear. Sometimes minke whales will breach clear of the water, on occasion many times in sequence.

Minke whales are generally seen as anything from single animals to several, but in areas of plankton abundance there may be a feeding assembly of a thousand or so. They take plankton and also squid. In turn they may be attacked by killer whales.

Minke males are sexually mature when they reach a length of about 7.2–7.7m (23–25ft), and females at 7.9–8.1m (26–27ft), and are seven or eight years old. Gestation takes 10–11 months, with the calves weaned in six months. Migratory movements are little known, but the animals travel south to equatorial waters to avoid the boreal winter. Larger animals penetrate further north in the summer, while non-breeders, calves and immatures stay to the south.

The total world population of minkes may be in the order of a quarter of a million, leading to claims that exploitation is sustainable, but the northern population has suffered grievous over-exploitation in the past. They are fished by Norwegians, who claim the stocks are well able to withstand the harvest. Both economic considerations and public opinion will decide their future in the long-term.

Minke whale. From Sir William Jardine, 'The Naturalist's Library', vol VIII, London, 1839

BOWHEAD
(Greenland right whale)
Balaena mysticetus

Although a truly Arctic species, the bowhead is decidedly uncommon. Linnaeus gave it its scientific name from the Greek *mustax*, 'moustache', and *ketos*, 'sea monster'; 'bowhead' comes from its bow-shaped skull.

An average bowhead grows up to 15m in length and weighs between 50 and 100 tonnes. It has a very large mouth equipped with the longest of all baleen plates found among the world's whales: they may be up to 4m long. It has no dorsal fin, presumably to make life easier when swimming under ice. In surfacing to breathe, it tends to show two distinct curves in profile as it reveals itself for the double blow half a dozen times in two or three minutes, before sounding for 20 minutes. The tail flukes are thrown high as it slides under maybe to 500m. On occasion bowheads may lift their massive heads clear of the water, showing a white bib.

Bowheads move north in the spring as high as 75°N when the ice breaks up. They then give birth, the Canadian population off Baffin Island, the Norwegian Sea animals perhaps around Jan Mayen. They are slow

Length
12–18m
(40–60ft)

Weight
50–100 tonnes

'The mighty whale
doth in these harbours
lye, Whose oyl the
careful merchant
deare will buy'
William Morrell,
'A brief narration
of the Ayre, Earth,
Water, Fish and
Fowles',
London, 1625

*Gun harpoon from
'An Account of the
Arctic Regions',
William Scoresby,
Constable, 1820*

swimmers, feeding on surface plankton at about three knots, working the edge of the pack, feeding in baleen whale fashion on vast quantities of plankton invertebrates, sieved through the 'whalebone' plates which hang from their upper jaws. Fine fringes on the baleen plates strain the water out from great gulps of sea as the huge tongue presses against them, retaining the catch of krill, copepods and pteropods between tongue and baleen to be swallowed. Mating takes place between June and August; the gestation period is ten months and the calves are suckled for a year. In summertime the whales may be seen close in to the coast and fjords of Svalbard. As the ice advances, they migrate south to winter as far down as 55°N.

Their great size and the fact that they float when killed made bowheads desirable prey for early whalers (a preferred catch in the days before compressed air was used to keep whale carcasses afloat). Originally abundant in Greenland waters, they were heavily exploited from the 17th century. Now there are only remnants in the Davis Strait/Baffin Bay area, although were lucky enough to see a party of at least 50 in the Foxe Basin in September 2011. The greatest number is confined to the Chukchi Sea, where there may be some 7,000 or so. In Franz Josef Land and around Svalbard there may be less than a hundred individuals. On Amsterdam Island, off the northwest of Spitsbergen, you may still see the remains of the ovens set up by the Dutch whalers, who established what developed into a whaling town in the 17th century. Whaling flourished there for 50 years (see page 12).

The long decline in their numbers eventually led to the end of bowhead whaling after the turn of the 19th century, when faster boats and improved harpoons made it possible to chase the fast-swimming minke whales. Bowhead whaling had effectively ended by 1912. In spite of having been protected for over 90 years (native subsistence hunting accounts for only a few – Inuit say they make the finest *muktuk*), the population is only now increasing. There may be 1,200 individuals in the Disko region of Greenland. Bowheads are an endangered species, yet it has been shown that an individual may live more than 200 years.

SPERM WHALE
(Cachalot)
Physeter macrocephalus

Once the main quarry of whalers, the sperm whale is large and unmistakable, dark grey, sometimes blotched white, with a huge boxy head more than a third of its length, on top of a narrow underslung jaw which seems out of proportion – the classic 'great whale' of literature and illustration. (*White* sperm whales – as in *Moby Dick* – do occur, but are rare.) It has no dorsal fin, but two thirds of the way down the back there is a marked dorsal hump, followed by a series of knuckles reaching to the tail. Flippers are short. On surfacing, the massive head exposes the single blowhole, which is placed well on the port side, resulting in a biased blow which is characteristically well off centre and forward in direction. The offset blow is unique to sperm whales. The blow is explosive and can be heard at a great distance.

Most dives last about ten minutes followed by about ten blows at intervals of 10–15 seconds, but dives can extend to well over an hour. In sounding, the sperm whale rolls to reveal the hump and then lifts the tail fluke high into the air in the manner of a humpback. They normally surface in the same place as they sound, the dive taking place vertically down and up.

The surface cruising speed is about 3 knots; on a dive it increases to 4 knots going down, then on the

Average length:
males 15m (50ft)
females 11m (36ft)

Average weight:
males 40 tonnes
females 22 tonnes

Note forward blow

View from behind showing spout asymmetry

Diving view

upward journey it reaches 5 knots. In search of giant squid, sperm whales dive regularly to 1,000m (3,281ft). They eat up to a tonne each day. They have been tracked by sonar to nearly 3,000m (9,843ft) – a bottom-dwelling shark was taken from a whale stomach where the depth was more than 3,200m (10,500ft). It is possible that the brilliantly white interior of the whale's mouth, in conjunction with the carmine tongue, acts as a lure, the whale simply opening its mouth and waiting for fish and squid to enter the trap. Around their heads they often have circular scars, sucker marks from the tentacles of the giant squid.

Sperm whales are widely distributed throughout the seven seas, always in deep water, but only the males penetrate into polar waters, in the summertime, when they may be found right up to the pack-ice but not inside it. They are often alone, sometimes in small groups.

Factory-ship whaling is now prohibited but sperm whales are still taken at shore stations in Iceland and Japan. Their products of oil, spermaceti and meal go mainly to industry.

SPERMACETI

Spermaceti is a clear liquid wax which is found in the 'melon' – the massive forehead of the animal. It is contained in a 'case', and together they serve as a hydrostatic device which controls buoyancy. It is also speculated that the curious arrangements in the sperm whale's head associated with the spermaceti act as a kind of acoustic parabolic reflector, and that the undoubtedly violent noises this whale can produce may be used to stun their prey.

Taken from the whale and cooled, spermaceti sets as a white wax which accounts for the analogy with semen (spermaceti translates literally as 'whale semen').

AMBERGRIS

Ambergris is a pliable yellowy-brown wax-like substance which forms around squid beaks in the stomach of the sperm whale, rather in the manner of a hairball. Lighter than water, it melts at about 65°C and dissolves readily in absolute alcohol or vegetable oils. It has been used for centuries as a vehicle to retain and prolong the scent of perfume. Long prized as an aphrodisiac in the orient, its use in expensive perfumes (although synthetics are available) is logical enough.

NORTHERN BOTTLENOSE WHALE

Hyperoodon ampullatus

Largest of the beaked whales, the northern bottlenose is found only in the colder latitudes of the North Atlantic, from the Davis Strait to the Barents Sea. A sickle-shaped dorsal fin is set well back on the body but the most striking characteristic is the dolphin-like beak and bulbous melon. The mainly dark-grey body is relieved as it ages by a distinctly paler forehead in the case of the male, whereas the female enjoys a whitish collar.

Most populations are migratory, ranging high to the edge of the ice in summer. Preferring deep water, this sociable species tends to be in small groups, rarely more than ten, although a resident population of some 200 lives year-round in the region of the Gully, a submarine canyon off Nova Scotia. Sexually mature from about nine, they mate in late spring/early summer. The gestation period is 12 months.

They are curious in the vicinity of ships and unusual noises, and are likely to come close to investigate if a

Length
males to 9.8m (32ft)
females to 8.7m (29ft)

Weight
5,800 to 7,500kg
(13,000 to 17,000lb)

vessel is lying in the water, engines stopped but generator running. They may breach or they may lobtail, showing the diagnostic lack of a notch between the flukes. They may lie on the surface for several minutes at a time, with a forward-facing bushy blow every half-minute or so. Between blows they cruise; melon, back and fin all visible at the same time.

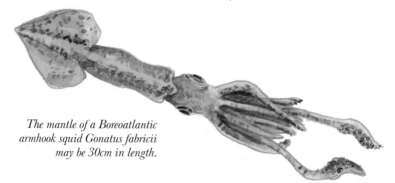

After several minutes they raise flukes and dive. Normally a dive lasts perhaps a quarter of an hour but whalers recorded them being down for up to an hour, probably under stress. They may dive to 800m (2,600ft) with a probable maximum at 1,500m (5,000ft) in pursuit of squid *Gonatus fabricii*. Bottom-feeders like starfish may be taken to a lesser extent as well as fish like herrings. They share with sperm whales production of the waxy spermaceti in their great heads, which made them attractive to the early whalers who regarded them as an easy catch. Hunted in large numbers from the mid-18th century, they were in serious decline until protection in 1973. They winter as far south as Maine in the west and Cape Verde in the east. Strandings, sometimes in groups, are not uncommon, from Newfoundland to Norway.

The mantle of a Boreoatlantic armhook squid Gonatus fabricii may be 30cm in length.

NARWHAL
(Unicorn)
Monodon monoceros

'A Sea monster, having a horne, had therewith stricken against the Ship, with most great strength. For when we set the ship on the Strand to make it cleane, about seven feet under water wee found a Horne sticking in the Ship, much like for thickness and fashion to a common Elephant's tooth, not hollow, but full, very strong hard Bone, which had entered into three Plankes of the Ship, that is two thicke Planes of Greene, and one of Oken Wood, and so into a Rib, where it turned upward, to our great good fortune. It struck at least halfe a foote deepe into the Ship.'

Richard Hakluyt, *Purchas his Pilgrimes*, 1624

The narwhal is one of the world's most striking animals, and it spawned, by virtue of its long, spiralling tusk, one of the most charming myths – that of the unicorn. Linnaeus was having nothing of myth and classified it from the Greek *monodon* (meaning 'one tooth') and *monoceros* ('one horn') a prosaic but almost precise description. Only the male sports the tusk, the longest of which was recorded at 2.7m in length. It emerges from a hole in the left side of the upper lip, spiralling clockwise, and totally straight. In fact there are two teeth, but they only rarely both erupt into tusks. Breaking the water's surface to blow at intervals of about a minute the tusk is revealed first, followed by a blotched back with no dorsal fin.

Length
5m max
(16.4ft)

Weight
1,600kg max
(3,528lb)

Narwhals are confined to west Greenland and the Canadian Arctic, and are most abundant in the Baffin Island/Lancaster Sound area on the western side of the Davis Strait. In the spring, migration occurs off Bylot Island where there may be as many as 30,000 individuals. Usually, however, they are found in small single-sex gams.

The function of the tusk has been the subject of much controversy, though it seems clear that as a male characteristic it is used in establishing dominance in sexual rivalry. 'Crossing swords' may sometimes be in play, but at courting time in spring the tusk is used as a weapon and fights are frequent – sometimes the tip of the tusk is broken. Its use in fishing is less clear. It has been suggested that the animal spears fish with it, but how would it then get them into its mouth? Much more likely is that the tusk makes furrows through the bottom sediment, flushing flatfish. The tusks become worn at the tip, supporting this theory. However, the female narwhal, which has no tusk, fishes effectively and survives perfectly well without one. Flounders are certainly preyed on by narwhals, and they also take squid, crustaceans and Arctic cod.

Mating takes place in March to May; the gestation period is 15 months, with calves being born the following summer. Females produce young every three years during their fertile years and the calf is nursed for two years. Young males begin to sprout their tusks at one year.

For centuries narwhals were hunted with harpoons for the tusks of ivory, which had great value as spears, as status symbols and, in theory at least, as aphrodisiacs. Today they are taken in strict quota by the Inuit, who market them with tags proving they were shot under licence. To export a tusk from the Inuit region of Nunavut it is necessary to have a permit. The Inuit have always used the red narwhal meat to feed their sled dogs; they use the sinews for sewing thread and process the blubber into the delicacy *muktuk*.

BELUGA
(White whale, sea canary)
Delphinapterus leucas

Truly Arctic, the beluga (Russian for 'white one') is a small whale found in Arctic Canada, Greenland, Svalbard and Russia. It weighs over a tonne and averages about 4.5m (14.8ft) in length. The beluga is the easiest of all whales to identify by its pure white colour, although this yellows with age. Rotund and robust, the beluga is a sociable creature, rarely alone, and relatively common around the ice. Regarded as a shallow-water whale, it nevertheless spends much time diving in deep water. It is not uncommon around the fjords of West Spitsbergen, but the best chance of finding a beluga is in the Davis Strait and around Baffin Island in the Canadian Arctic. There is a sedentary population in the St Lawrence river. The easiest place of all to see them is in Hudson Bay, in July to August, when 3,000 congregate in the Churchill River.

*Length
3.5–4.5m
(11.5–14.8ft)*

*Weight
1,700kg max
(3,748lb)*

Beluga caviar comes not from the whale but from the roe of the European sturgeon Huso huso, of the Caspian and Black seas.

Typically, belugas swim steadily along the surface, unlike most other whales, breathing in a rather thin steamy burst a couple of times a minute. They spend a lot of time under the pack ice, with the broad and flexible head used as a cushion to lift the floes in order to breathe. They can break through as much as 100cm of solid ice.

They are a talkative species – a 'gam' of belugas would be the perfect description for a pod whose species was known to whalers as the sea canary because of its varied and musical vocabulary. They indulge in trills, clicks, squeals, bell sounds, whistles and raspberries, sounds which are heard clearly above the surface.

Pods of a dozen or so belugas consist normally of either males or females with calves, though they may gather in literally thousands to calve and mate. The gestation period is 12–14 months. Summering in the high Arctic, the single calf is born in July in the relatively warm shallow waters of estuaries and fjords. Dark grey-brown at birth, the calf is nursed for more than a year and may remain close to its mother for years, becoming white when it is sexually mature.

Unlike the narwhal, the beluga's teeth do not erupt; it has 34 simple pegs in a large mouth. In their main feeding period belugas work in deep water, diving to as much as 600m/1,968ft (the deepest recorded is 872m/2,860ft) for up to 20 minutes at a time to nuzzle in the silt for invertebrates, bottom fish such as halibut, and capelin, char, cod and lanternfish. Summering in the high Arctic, they migrate south in spectacular numbers to winter.

Protected in Svalbard since 1955, belugas are to this day prey for the Inuit, in whose Canadian territory they are still taken legally. Easily trapped by their requirement to visit breathing holes, their skin is prized for the delicacy *muktuk*, which is chewed raw, boiled or smoked, and their almost transparent blubber is used as a fuel oil for lamps. Although there is some doubt as to whether the species is still viable, the world population is estimated at somewhere between 100,000 and 200,000. They may live for up to 30 years, possibly 40.

KILLER WHALE
(Orca, demon dolphin, blackfish)
Orcinus orca

Orcinus 'bringer of death'
orca 'sea monster'

Killers are cosmopolitan and common, found in coastal areas throughout the seven seas. The name has given them an undeservedly vicious reputation, so much so that there are those who try to sanitise them with the name 'orca'. But killers they are, taking penguins, seals, fish and, on occasion, other whales. There are no records yet of them taking tourists though they are perfectly capable of overturning an ice floe in order to topple a sleeping seal into their jaws. They are commonly at home among the pack ice, especially near seabird colonies and concentrations of seals.

Length
males to 9.5m
(30ft)
females to 7m
(23ft)

Weight
males to 7 tonnes
females to 3.5 tonnes

The largest of the dolphins, with a blunt head, the killer whale is strikingly jet black above and brilliant white below, with a grey saddle behind the dorsal fin, a diagnostic white ellipse behind and above the eye, and a white incursion from the belly into the flanks behind and below the saddle. The dorsal fin is highly distinctive. In the female it is sickle-shaped and stands tall, but in the male it is triangular, reaching to almost 2m (6ft), and is unmistakable, even from a great distance.

They are curious and interested in ships, likely to change course and approach to cavort around and under a vessel which behaves with respect. They may also display interest by 'spyhopping' – rising vertically in the water as high as their paddle-shaped flippers in order to view the scene and search for likely prey. They may slap the water with their tails – 'lobtailing'. 'Breaching' clear of the water is behaviour common in northern waters but not yet recorded in the Antarctic. They can swim at great speed on the surface, though normally they cruise as a close-knit group, often in line abreast. They dive for several minutes, followed by a breathing sequence of a few 10–30 second shallow dives. They tend to travel in small family groups – pods – with a well-developed social structure, in which the dominant male is easily recognised by his tall fin. Pods may comprise anything from a few to a couple of dozen or more animals. A pod normally contains one dominant adult male, several breeding females, and juveniles of both sexes.

Clear photos showing dorsal fins, saddle and/or eye patches will be much appreciated and acknowledged by the Orca Research Trust, P O Box 1233, Whangarei, New Zealand. Sighting sheets from www.orcaresearch.org

THE BERING SEA

Stretching between 56 and 66°N, from the Aleutians to the Chukchi Sea and Wrangel Island, the Bering Sea, by virtue of remaining within the 10°C summer isotherm, comes within the scope of this book and is biologically Arctic. As the ice retreats, these waters offer rich plankton fishing in the summer over a wide continental shelf for species which are not normally seen elsewhere in the Arctic. They add spice to an Arctic list. In commercial terms, they provide half of the US marine harvest. This appendix reveals some of the likely sightings.

Vitus Bering was a Danish-born Russian navigator employed by Peter the Great to sail from Kamchatka in 1728 to discover and confirm the separation of the continents of Asia and America.

141

PLANTS

Wild plants resistant to salt and wind thrive in the warmer microclimate between huge boulders multi-coloured with moss and lichen. They are much valued for the pot.

Monkshood, *Aconitum delphinifolium*, tall blue-purple spikes. Yields a poison formerly used by Aleutian hunters, who dipped their spears in a concentrated extract to tranquilise sea mammals.

Narcissus anemone, *Anemone narcissiflora*, used as cress in salads. Prepared in blubber oil and beaten to a creamy consistency for Eskimo ice cream.

Arctic scurvy-grass, *Cochlearia fenestrata*, leaves rich in vitamin C, historically valuable to sailors in danger of suffering from scurvy.

Cloudberry, *Rubus chamaemorus*, sensitive to salt and to dry conditions but can withstand temperatures down to well below −40°C. Bogs, marshes and wet meadows in acidic ground. Ripe fruit yellow/orange and delicious.

Arctic fireweed (dwarf rosebay willowherb), *Epilobium latifolium*, source of vitamins C and A. The young shoots are delicious with bacon. Leaves as a form of tea (Kapor). Provides honey and syrups, jellies.

PINK SALMON
(Humpback)
Oncorhynchus gorbuscha

Feeding on shrimp and krill, the primary name of this fish comes from the resulting 'salmon pink' of the flesh. The 'humpy' is the smallest and most abundant of Pacific salmon, perfectly at home in the cold waters of the north. Maturing in two years, it is while on migration to the spawning grounds that the male fish develops the laterally flattened hump. Its range is from the Lena River in Siberia to the Bering Sea, where it may be seen in summer spawning in coastal waters, even in the intertidal zone. Both parents die within a week or two after spawning. Pink salmon roe has become a valuable export to Asia as 'caviar'.

Length
males to 63cm
(25in)

COHO SALMON
(Silver salmon)
O. Krsutch

After their first couple of years in fresh water the smolts enter the ocean, where they become the backbone of the Alaskan troll fishery, much prized for the table because of their high fat content. Spawning at three years, the males develop the characteristic hooked snout and impressive teeth, at which stage they are called kypes. The black spots which are sprinkled across the back are smaller than those of the pink salmon. Their range is from California to the Bering Sea. Native tribes have used this species in trade.

Length
males to 75cm
(30in)

SHORT-TAILED SHEARWATER
Puffinus tenuirostris

The most abundant shearwater in the Bering and Chukchi seas, the short-tailed shearwater is to be seen at sea in summer flocks of sometimes tens of thousands, after a long-haul migration from the breeding grounds of the Antipodes. (Sooty shearwaters tend to be in similar numbers, but mostly south of the Aleutians.) It is dark at a distance, but catch it as it flies by and there is a silvery undersheen. Closer, there are large irregular whitish patches over most of the underwing. (Sooties exhibit a more regular dark brown.) Plunge-dives and surface snatches for small fish and squid.

Length
40–45cm
(16–18in)

Wingspan
95–100cm
(37–39in)

FORK TAILED STORM-PETREL
Oceanodroma furcata

The only pearl-grey storm-petrel, this is whitish below. A confirmed ship-follower, it is often seen at night as a pale and ghostly shape as it flies past the wheelhouse window or a porthole near water level. They are attracted by the ship's lights at night, when squid come to the surface. During the day they take small fish. The forked tail is not easy to see except from above, but the fluttering, darting and fast erratic flight is characteristic. The only other small birds which they might be confused with at sea are the phalaropes, but they helpfully fly in straight lines. In late summer the storm-petrels may often be seen close to the shore.

Native hunters called them oilbirds from the way in which they consorted with whales, enjoying the fruit of their oily breath.

Length
20–23cm
(8–9in)

Wingspan
46cm
(18in)

HARLEQUIN DUCK
Histrionicus histrionicus

Summer portrait

These are sea ducks hardened to a life in turbulent, cold waters. Strikingly decorated, the drake is mostly slate blue, spotted and striped white with chestnut flanks. The duck is suitably drab for camouflage at nesting time, when she chooses a well-sheltered place in dense vegetation or under rocks, never far from a fast-flowing stream nor the open sea. Once the ducklings are fit, the family moves to the coast, joining others in a sociable flock. Hugging an exposed and rocky coast, unabashed by heavy surf and crashing waves, they dive, using the short but powerful bill to dislodge molluscs and crustaceans. With a layer of air under their dense plumage they are exceptionally buoyant, but also well insulated against the cold. In conversation, accustomed to noisy conditions, they rely on high-pitched squeaks and whistles, unlike more conventional duck quacking.

Harlequins are not inclined to migration; they remain to winter around these inhospitable waters. The coast of the Bering Sea is their stronghold, and maybe a million breed in the Aleutians, plus perhaps 3,000 in northern Iceland.

Length
38–45cm
(15–18in)

Wingspan
63–69cm
(25–27in)

…and in
winter plumage

RED-LEGGED KITTIWAKE
Rissa brevirostris

The Bering Sea is home to the world's entire breeding population of red-legged kittiwakes – perhaps 100,000 pairs. Sadly their numbers are declining and they are a decidedly vulnerable species. Reasons for the decline are not too clear, but changes in food supply, increased predation by foxes and commercial trawling are probably involved. While they once normally laid two or three eggs, they now seem to stick at one. They are not yet formally protected.

Length
36–38cm
(14–15in)

Wingspan
90cm
(35in)

Black-legged kittiwakes, which are well distributed around the Arctic and sub-Arctic coasts, are well established in this region too, and the redlegs share their exposed cliffs.

They plunge or dip for small fish and squid over the edge of the shelf. At the end of the breeding season they move south, ahead of the advancing ice.

PIGEON GUILLEMOT
Cepphus columba

The pigeon guillemot is common in the Bering Sea, its stronghold, especially in the Chukotsky Peninsula. Although it often congregates in small colonies, it is less obviously sociable than other auks. Its black-brown body with a distinctive white patch broken by black wedges distinguishes it from the black guillemot, which overlaps with it at the northern end of its range. It has elegant red legs and a black bill with a red mouth. It makes its home along a rocky coastline with cliffs and slopes offering crevices and cavities for nest sites. Unlike other auks, it always stays close to inshore shallow waters, where it dives to scour the bottom for molluscs and crustaceans.

Length
34cm
(13.5in)

Wingspan
58cm
(23in)

AUKS

MARBLED MURRELET
Brachyramphus perdix

Length 25cm (9.75in)
Wingspan 40cm (16in)

The breeding arrangements of the nocturnal murrelets are not well known; in the case of Kittlitz's, hardly at all. But they are common at sea and along the coast, although hard to tell apart. Marbled murrelets are darker down to the waterline; Kittlitz's, which are much more common in the northern part of the Bering Sea, are mottled golden-brown and lighter round the waterline, and show a white tail when flushed. Murrelets forage close inshore, diving for small stuff. In flight they are fast and enjoy a rocking motion.

KITTLITZ'S MURRELET
B. brevirostris

Length 24cm (9.5in)
Wingspan 43cm (17in)

PARAKEET AUKLET
Aethia psittacula

Length 25cm (10in) Wingspan 45cm (18in)

A dumpy bird with an upturned reddish bill. It has a direct flight over the water in shallow offshore waters, diving for crustaceans. Flocks tend to gather on the surface for evening discussions.

CRESTED AUKLET
A. cristatella

Length 23cm (9in) Wingspan 43cm (17in)

Slate-grey, with a stubby orange bill and an impressive thick crest. Highly developed flocking behaviour, indulging in sensational aerial displays, clouding the evening sky.

LEAST AUKLET
A. pusilla

Length 16cm (6.25in) Wingspan 30.5cm (12in)

It may be tiny, but this is perhaps the most abundant seabird in the Bering Sea. Foraging offshore, they collect copepods in a gular pouch, dovekie style, delivering several meals a day to the chick on its remote coast or island. Where there is no shortage of suitable nest-crevices, a colony may hold a million birds.

HORNED PUFFIN
Fratercula corniculata

Length
38cm
(15in)

Wingspan
58cm
(23in)

Both Pacific puffins have white faces; the horned puffin has a black collar but is white underneath whereas the rest of the tufted puffin is all black. Horned puffins have a large triangular orange-red and yellow bill, but you need to be very close to see the fleshy 'horn' above the eye. Tufteds have an orange bill and long yellowish tufts hanging back from the eye.

Both are common and abundant on sea coasts and offshore islands in the Bering Sea/Aleutian region. They are comfortable in mixed colonies as they are not in competition for nest sites. Horned puffins choose to nest in cliff crevices or under boulders in the talus slopes, while tufted puffins burrow into grassy slopes, even to the top of an island. They may dig as much as 2m into the soil and have two entrances.

On the whole, puffins prefer to fly underwater rather than in air. Diving to chase for small fish they use their wings for propulsion, and their orange legs as control surfaces.

TUFTED PUFFIN
F. cirrhata

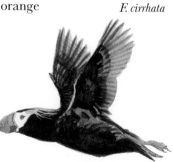

Length
38cm
(15in)

Wingspan
63cm
(25in)

NORTHERN FUR SEAL
Callorhinus ursinus

Largest of the world's fur seals, the stocky bulls are much larger than the cows. Total population is well over a million, of which two thirds are found around the Pribilofs and the Commander Islands. The older males are first to arrive in May at the ancestral rookery in order to lay claim to the prime breeding places, the females following and giving birth soon after. The males fast throughout the season, mating with their harem of anything up to a hundred females. Young males hang around close to the action, watching for a chance to score. Pups are weaned by October.

They dive to 180m (600ft) for pelagic fish and squid. Today their main predators are killer whales, though juveniles are prey for arctic foxes and even sea lions, but in the past they were taken first by natives, and then by Europeans, in huge numbers for meat and for their fur. The luxuriant pelage was the focus of a thriving trade in the 19th and early 20th centuries, which brought the species to its knees before it was saved by one of the first international treaties devoted to wildlife conservation. Having retreated to this northerly part of its range it has recovered, but there is current concern, as pup production in the Pribilofs has been decreasing.

Length
males to 2m
females to 1.3m

Weight
males to 275kg
(600lb)
females to 50kg
(110lb)

NORTHERN SEA LION
(Steller sea lion)
Eumetopias jubatus

*Length
males to 3.25m
(10½ft)
females to 2.5m
(8¼ft)*

*Weight
males to 1,100kg
(2,420lb)
females to 300kg
(660lb)*

*Georg Wilhelm Steller
sailed as naturalist on
Bering's second
Kamchatka expedition.
He described the sea
lion for science in 1742
when shipwrecked on
Bering Island.*

This is almost the largest of all eared seals – only the walrus is larger. The males are robust, with a short blunt snout and an impressive mane. The females are blonder and smaller. Like the fur seal but unlike the true seals, the sea lion can rotate its hind flippers, lift itself up upon its fore flippers and run.

Their breeding range is similar to that of the fur seal, with traditional rookeries congregating on the rocky shores of isolated islands, where the males are highly aggressive, holding territories where females are not held in a harem but have a degree of freedom to wander. Male battles are usually brief.

They are deep divers for fish and squid. In the past they were taken for food and clothes, and more recently pups were taken in numbers. There is still a subsistence harvest by native Americans but their abundance has suffered serious decline for reasons which are not clear. Commercial overfishing may be partly to blame.

GREY WHALE
Eschrichtius robustus

The mottled grey/white body distinguishes the grey whale from other whales. Its tapered head leads to a robust body. It has no dorsal fin, but merely a hump and a string of knuckles.

Calving in the warm lagoons of Baja California, grey whales reach the cold water feeding grounds of the Bering Sea in the summer after an impressive 8,000km coastal migration.

They are bottom feeders, sucking sediment and filtering small crustaceans and tubeworms through baleen. Dives last three to five minutes, maybe longer, in relatively shallow water, and whales often show flukes on diving. There may be a trail of mud in the wake of a foraging whale. They also take mid-water fish. The 4m blow is bushy or heart-shaped. It breaches and spyhops.

Grey whales, now confined to the North Pacific, were once widespread in the northern hemisphere. They were heavily exploited in the past (called devilfish by whalers on account of their ferocity) but have been fully protected since 1947, though subject to aboriginal hunting in waters off Chukotka. They are no longer regarded as endangered, and their total population may be 23,000. The average lifespan is 30 to 40 years, but they may live to 60.

Length to 15m (49ft)

Weight to 35,000kg (77,000lb)

Spyhopping

Arctic Code of Conduct

Those who travel in polar regions should know that the environment in these areas is especially vulnerable. Birds, mammals and plants are all surviving in the marginal existence zone. Because of seasonal light and low air and water temperatures, life processes are slower, particularly in plant recovery rates. The following general rules should be observed when ashore:

- Avoid unnecessary damage to the ground surface and vegetation cover, as regeneration rates are extremely slow. Do not take specimens from plants.

- Avoid disturbing or feeding the wildlife. Be aware of your activities and whether they are resulting in a change of the animals' behaviour. Disturbance of some animals may lead to aggressive behaviour. Be aware that rabies does occur in Arctic foxes.

- Be careful when moving in areas where birds are nesting. If birds are disturbed and leave their nests, the uncovered eggs cool quickly and are easy prey for gulls and foxes.

- In the summer, geese and some other duck species moult their wing feathers. In this condition they are unable to fly and are particularly vulnerable. Avoid accidentally herding or alarming them as this can split the flocks and encourage predators.

- Cultural monuments and items such as burial sites, crosses, coins, weapons, hunting tools, etc are regularly encountered. Such cultural monuments are generally protected by law. It is unlawful to destroy or remove such monuments and items from the place where they are found.

- Leave no litter ashore and remove any litter you may find while ashore. Do not take souvenirs, including whale or seal bones, live or dead animals, rocks, fossils, plants, or other organic material.

GLOSSARY OF SNOW AND ICE

Anchor ice Submerged ice which is attached to the bottom.

Bergy bit A piece of floating ice, generally showing less than 5m (16ft) above sea level but more than 1m (3ft), and normally about 10m (32ft) across.

Bight An extensive crescent-shaped indentation in the ice edge, formed either by wind or current.

Brash ice Accumulations of floating ice made up of fragments not more than 2m (6ft) across the wreckage of other forms of ice.

Bergy bit

Calving The breaking away of a mass of ice from an ice wall, ice front or iceberg.

Crevasse A fissure formed in a glacier; often hidden by snow bridges.

Fast-ice Sea-ice which forms and remains fast along the coast, where it is attached to the shore, to an ice wall, to an ice front, over shoals or between grounded icebergs. May extend a few metres or several hundred kilometres from the shore. May be more than one year old. When surface level is higher than 2m (6ft) above sea level it is called an ice shelf.

Fast-ice

Firn Old snow which has recrystallised into a dense material.

Floe Floating ice other than fast-ice or glacier ice.

Frazil ice Fine spicules or plates of ice, suspended in water.

Frost smoke Fog-like clouds due to contact of cold air with relatively warm water, which can appear over openings in the ice or leeward of the ice edge, and which may persist while ice is forming.

Glacier A mass of snow and ice continuously moving to lower ground or, if afloat, continuously spreading.

Glacier

Grease ice A later stage of freezing than frazil ice when the crystals have coagulated to form a soupy layer on the surface. Grease ice reflects little light, giving the sea a matt appearance.

Growler A piece of ice almost awash, smaller than a bergy bit.

Hummock A mound or hillock of broken floating ice forced upwards by pressure. May be fresh or weathered. The submerged volume of broken ice under the hummock, forced downward by pressure, is a bummock.

Pinnacled iceberg

Iceberg A massive piece of ice of greatly varying shape, protruding more than 5m (16ft) above sea level. Icebergs may be described as tabular, dome-shaped, sloping, pinnacled, weathered or glacier bergs.

Ice blink A white glare on the underside of low clouds, indicating the presence of pack-ice or an ice sheet.

Icefoot A narrow fringe of ice attached to the coast, unmoved by tides and remaining after the fast-ice has broken free.

Lead A navigable passage through floating ice.

Moraine Ridges or deposits of rock debris transported by a glacier: lateral, along the sides; medial, down the centre; end, deposited at the foot.

Nilas

Nilas A thin crust of floating ice, easily bending on waves and swell and rafting under pressure. It has a matt surface and is up to 10cm (4in) thick. Under 5cm (2in) it is dark, more than 5cm (2in), lighter.

Nip Ice is said to nip when it forcibly presses against a ship. A vessel so caught, though undamaged, is said to have been nipped.

Nunatak A rocky crag or small mountain projecting from and surrounded by a glacier or ice sheet.

Old ice Sea-ice more than two years old, up to 3m (10ft) or more thick.

Pack-ice, open Composed of floes seldom in contact and with many leads. Ice cover 4/10 to 6/10.

close Pack-ice in which the concentration is 7/10 to 8/10, composed of floes mostly in contact.

very close Pack-ice in which the floes are tightly packed but not frozen together, with little sea water visible. Ice cover practically 10/10.

consolidated Pack-ice in which the concentration is 10/10. The floes are frozen together and no water is visible.

Close pack-ice

Pancake ice Predominantly circular pieces of ice from 30cm (12in) to 3m (10ft) in diameter, and up to about 10cm (4in) in thickness, with raised rims due to the pieces striking against each other. Formed from the freezing together of grease ice, slush or shuga, or the breaking up of ice rind or nilas.

Polynya Any water area in pack or fast-ice other than a lead, not large enough to be called open water.

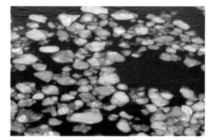

Pancake ice

Rafting Pressure process by which one floe overrides another; most commonly found in new and young ice.

Rotten ice Sea-ice which has become honeycombed in the course of melting and which is in an advanced state of disintegration.

Sastrugi Sharp, irregular ridges formed on a snow surface by wind erosion and deposition. The ridges are parallel to the direction of the prevailing wind.

Sea-ice Any form of ice found at sea which results from freezing sea water.

Shuga An accumulation of spongy white ice lumps, a few centimetres across, formed from grease ice or slush and sometimes from anchor ice rising to the surface.

Snow bridge An arch formed by snow which has drifted across a crevasse, forming first a corniche, and ultimately a covering which may completely obscure the opening.

Stranded ice Ice which has been floating and has been deposited on the shore by retreating high water.

Tongue A projection of the ice edge up to several kilometres in length, caused by wind or current.

'Out of whose womb came the ice? and the hoary frost of heaven, who hath gendered it? The waters are hid as with a stone, and the face of the deep is frozen.'

Job 38: 29

FURTHER READING

Once bitten by the Arctic bug – and like its Antarctic cousin it bites deep and doesn't let go – you will thirst for more sustenance. These books will go a long way to providing it.

Birkhead, Tim *Great Auk Islands* T & A D Poyser, 1993

Carwardine, Mark et al *Whales & Dolphins* HarperCollins, 1998

Densley, Michael *In Search of Ross's Gull* Peregrine Books, 1999

Evans, Polly *Northern Lights* Bradt, 2010

Hardy, Alister *The Open Sea* Collins New Naturalist, 1956

Harrison, Peter *Seabirds - An Identification Guide* Croom Helm, 1985

Lopez, Barry *Arctic Dreams* Macmillan, 1986

MacLean, Stephen *Familiar Plants of Coastal Alaska* Greatland Graphics, 2010

MacLean, Stephen *Svalbard Plants* Greatland Graphics, 2010

Madge, Steve & Burn, Hilary *Wildfowl* Christopher Helm, 1988

Martin, Tony *Beluga Whales,* Colin Baxter Photography Ltd, 1996

Mehlum, Fridtjof *The birds & mammals of Svalbard* Norwegian Polar Institute, 1990

Mountfield, David *Polar Exploration* Hamlyn, 1974

Ogilvie, M A *Ducks* T & A D Poyser, 1975

Pielou, EC *A Naturalist's Guide to the Arctic* University of Chicago Press, 1994

Reeves, Randall R et al *Sea Mammals of the World* A & C Black, 2002

Rønning, Olaf *The Flora of Svalbard* Norwegian Polar Institute, 1996

Sage, Bryan *The Arctic and its Wildlife* Croom Helm, 1986

Sale, Richard *A Complete Guide to Arctic Wildlife* Christopher Helm, 2006

Sale, Richard & Potapov, Eugene *The Scramble for the Arctic* Frances Lincoln, 2010

Savours, Ann *The Northwest Passage* Chatham, 2001

Scoresby, William *An Account of the Arctic Regions* Constable, 1820

Snow D W & Perrings C M *The Birds of the Western Palearctic* Oxford University Press, 1988

Stonehouse, Bernard *Animals of the Arctic: The ecology of the far north* Ward Lock, 1971

Stonehouse, Bernard *North Pole South Pole* Prion, 1990

Swaney, Deanna *The Arctic* Lonely Planet, 1999

Umbreit, Andreas *Spitsbergen: The Bradt Travel Guide* Bradt Travel Guides, 2005

Vaughan, Richard *In Search of Arctic Birds* T & A D Poyser, 1992

Wheeler, Sara *The Magnetic North* Vintage Books, 2010

INDEX

AUTHOR

Tony Soper is a wildlife film-maker and naturalist who has spent 20 years working his way round the wilderness islands of both polar regions. He has sailed as expedition leader on icebreakers and ice-hardened vessels in the Antarctic in the austral summer and in the Arctic in the northern summer. His enthusiasm for wildlife has been shared by a large number of willing expedition cruise guests. This book aims to answer some of their questions!

ILLUSTRATOR

Dan Powell has been a wildlife artist since graduating from Dyfed College of Art in Wales in 1983. He was honoured as British Birds Illustrator of the Year in 1996. His work has appeared in numerous books and journals, including many publications by the Royal Society for the Protection of Birds, on subjects ranging from parrots to dragonflies. He is happiest when out sketching in the field – especially when stuck in the middle of a bog.

ACKNOWLEDGEMENTS

Many people have given freely of their knowledge and polar experience in the preparation of this book. In particular we should like to thank Bob Headland, Bernard Stonehouse and Charles Swithinbank of the Scott Polar Research Institute in Cambridge and Rob Barrett of the University of the Arctic in Tromsø. Pat Toomey, of the Canadian Coastguard, masterminded a spectacular voyage by coupled icebreakers through the Northeast Passage. Ian Stone encouraged us to an understanding of the history of Arctic exploration; Katarina Salén, Ko de Korte, Rinie van Meurs, Kim Crosbie, Darrel Schoeling, Anna Sutcliffe, Richard White and Norm Lasca have all been the best of naturalist companions on expeditions to the wonderful wilderness islands ringing the Arctic Ocean.

None of this would have been possible without the skill of those professional seamen who venture to high northern latitudes with a cargo of wildlife enthusiasts. In particular we think of the skippers of the icebreakers *Kapitan Khlebnikov*, *Kapitan Dranitsyn*, *Yamal* and *Polarstar* and of RV *Professor Multanovsky*, MS *Clipper Adventurer* and MS *National Geographic Explorer*. To all those who have made it possible for us to enjoy the breathtaking beauty of the Arctic summer, we tender sincere thanks, and to all those who are lucky enough to be looking forward to a first exploration of the Arctic, we envy you!

T S www.tonysoper.com
D P www.powellwildlifeart.com

ENVOI

The Arctic wilderness is a significant part of our wild heritage, and it is a great privilege to be able to enjoy its hardy plants and abundant wildlife. In this book we have merely skimmed the surface in an introduction to the more obvious of its coastal and seagoing inhabitants. We have totally failed to address the immense problems which our species has wrought upon this fragile and vulnerable place. In exploring it, our ancestors exploited its whales and seals and fur-bearing animals mercilessly and without thought for the future. Perhaps we have learnt enough to look seals and whales and polar bears in the eye today with clearer consciences, but in turn we batter the Arctic with more sinister influences. Industrial developments, radioactive fallout, atmospheric and waterway pollution, and the ever-present danger of oil spill present a catalogue of ills which cry out for treatment, to say nothing about the consequences of climate change. Please go there and enjoy the beauty of it, but consider the need to join the ranks of those who work for a more intelligent attitude to the stewardship of our planet.

Worldwide fund for Nature www.wwf.panda.org
The Arctic Council www.arctic-council.org
Marine Conservation Society (UK) www.mcsuk.org
Association of Arctic Expedition Cruise Operators (AECO) www.aeco.no

> 'Strange. There is always sadness on departure. It is as if one cannot after all bear to leave this bleak waste of ice, glaciers, cold and toil...'
> Fridtjof Nansen, 1912